ARCHAEOLOGICAL
FINDS
A GUIDE TO IDENTIFICATION

ARCHAEOLOGICAL
FINDS

A GUIDE TO IDENTIFICATION

NORENA SHOPLAND

TEMPUS

ACKNOWLEDGEMENTS

This book is dedicated to my parents Pam and Bob Shopland with thanks for all their love and support.

My grateful thanks to the Treasure Trove of Scotland, particularly Jenny Shields, for permission to reproduce photographs here and to the Portable Antiquities Society for permission to reproduce images from their website.

To my dear friends Clair, Linda, Maxine and Sylvia for their unfailing support.

First published 2005

Tempus Publishing Limited
The Mill, Brimscombe Port,
Stroud, Gloucestershire, GL5 2QG
www.tempus-publishing.com

British Library Cataloguing in Publication Data.
A catalogue record for this book is available from the British Library.

ISBN 0 7524 3132 3

Typesetting and origination by Tempus Publishing Limited
Printed in Great Britain

CONTENTS

Introduction	7
Cleaning, drying and storing guidelines	9
Chapter 1 – Materials	13
Metals	14
Inorganics	37
Organics	41
Chapter 2 – Flint	59
Identifying worked flint	59
Flint choppers and axes	62
Flint flakes and flake tools	66
Flint cores	68
Flint blades and blade tools	71
Flint projectile points and arrowheads	75
Microliths	77
Gunflints	78
Pebble maceheads	79
Chapter 3 – Pottery	81
A guide to some pottery forms	81
Care of ceramics	87
Neolithic pottery	87
Bronze Age pottery	90
Iron Age pottery	91
Roman Samian ware	95
Roman Black Burnished ware	106
Roman Fine Ware beakers/cups	108
Roman Mortaria	109
Roman flagons	110
Roman amphorae	111
Anglo-Saxon pottery	115
Medieval pottery	117
Earthenware	121

Stoneware 122
Tin-glazed earthenware 125
Lead-glazed earthenware 126
Porcelain 128
Bone china 130
Dating pottery backstamps 131

Chapter 4 – Domestic Materials 135
Roman building material 135
Medieval roof tiles 138
Medieval floor tiles 141
Bricks 143
Glass wine bottles 146
Drinking glasses 151
Knives 156
Spoons 161
Forks 165
Hallmarks 167
Hones or whetstones 169
Bronze axes 170
Roman leather shoes 172
Saxon and medieval shoes 176
Roman brooches 179
Roman zoomorphic brooches 183
Roman hairpins 185
Hair combs 188
Pilgrim badges 190
Clay pipes 192
Dice 194
Medieval keys 196
Seal matrices 199
Horseshoes 203
Spurs 206
Thimbles 210
Pin beaters 212
Spindle whorls 213
Bone skates 216

Appendices
The Portable Antiquities Scheme 217
Treasure Trove of Scotland 219

Bibliography 223

INTRODUCTION

There is a vast literature dedicated to archaeological arte-facts. However, this information is generally spread throughout a myriad of papers and monographs. For those involved in dealing with finds in the field and in processing, there is no unified publication that may aid them in identifying and dating artefacts. When starting out in finds, I found the fastest way to learn was to ask others whose knowledge had been gained from years of experience. My main difficulty came when left alone for the first time as the only processor on a large inner-London site. Without others to turn to I resorted to photocopying large numbers of papers and pages from books to help me identify, date and take care of finds. From this I began to amass a large pile of photocopies which I then condensed into notes and illustrations which would serve as a quick reference. From those notes this book has emerged.

Artefacts are integral to the dating of any site and, given this importance, it therefore follows that any means by which those in the field can quickly identify and date finds makes the excavation process more efficient. This is particularly true not only of identification, but also of the care of finds as they are being removed from the ground, and as they are being processed.

Most finds are, of course, discovered in a partial state but it is hoped that by highlighting diagnostic features an attempt can be made at naming and dating an item, even if only partially recovered.

Obviously, the range of finds is vast and this book can only scratch the surface. The criterion for inclusion is frequency of recovery for a given type of artefact. In archaeological contexts, pottery and building material (and, at prehistoric sites, lithics) are always found. The frequency of recovery of items outside a formal archaeological context is more difficult to assess, and my simple choice would be too objective, so I consulted the Portable Antiquities Scheme and the Treasure Trove of Scotland. They kindly provided lists of the most frequent finds registered with them. The Portable Antiquities Scheme is responsible for the recording of all archaeological objects found by members of the public and gives a good overview of frequently found items. The Treasure Trove of Scotland, unlike the PAS, records all finds, regardless of whether they are metal detector finds or an archaeological excavation. These lists consisted of the top 100 most frequently found items. These items were then chosen according to their propensity to yield diagnostic features and ease of dating. Coins have not been included due to the fact that they usually carry monarchs' names or dates and inevitably would need a book of their own.

The pottery included here only features the most frequently recovered and gives enough information to identify those types. There is no intention here to teach typology or how to tell, say, Wedgwood from Spode. Instead this book provides guidelines on how to, for example, distinguish true porcelain from soft-paste porcelain. The main consideration throughout has been to enable readers to date artefacts, as this provides vital information in the field.

This is a vast subject and I apologise in advance for any errors which may have crept in. I would welcome any suggestions for improvements in future reprints.

CLEANING, DRYING AND STORING GUIDELINES

For the main text guidelines are given on appropriate cleaning techniques for each listing. However a few general comments regarding the cleaning of all finds are appropriate here.

Before cleaning any artefact, remove lids or loose items. Never lift an object by its handles, knobs, rims or other protuberances. The object may look stable but there may be hidden weaknesses, particularly as protrusions often suffer the first damage, and these weaknesses may be placed under stress if not sufficiently supported. Instead use both hands around the base or similar substantial area of the piece. Give the item a quick examination for cracks, weaknesses or repairs and be sure not to place these under stress when lifting and setting an object down.

When a piece has been stable in the ground for an extensive period, corrosion will often be stabilised. When that piece is removed from its context the effect on it can be sudden and corrosion, if present, may be accelerated. Therefore, be vigilant for any colour or texture change (such as the light, powdery green on bronze which may indicate bronze disease (see page 19)). If there are obvious changes, the corrosion process has begun and it is important to take quick action to prevent the piece deteriorating any further. With composite items certain areas may corrode more quickly than others – when this happens, conserve the item according to the material most at risk (if in doubt consult a conservator). Some composite items may have evidence of other materials in staining alone, such as rust marks: in these cases do not clean the area as the evidence will be removed. All metals, with the exception of gold, are subject to corrosion. Corrosion can alter the shape, colour and weight of an object and with some items, particularly iron, it may be extremely difficult to recognise the original item. It might be necessary to x-ray the piece in order to identify the shape. If in doubt do not clean off too much of the corrosion layer as it is often only this that holds the outline of where the object had once been.

Washing

Never wash a small find under a running tap as this may damage it, particularly if it is a composite one with organic or fragile parts which could be dislodged (this does not include bulk finds which are often power sprayed; however, vigilance when spraying is always necessary).

Do not leave finds to soak in water. Old repairs could become loose and any porous parts (such as feet on pottery which have not been glazed) will absorb water.

Do not use soaps or cleaning agents, as if they are not completely removed the chemicals in the soap may corrode the artefact. Clean tepid water should be enough to clean most finds.

When using abrasive brushes, such as toothbrushes, be particularly vigilant for loose parts on the artefact.

Do not use toothbrushes on soft items, particularly earthenware pottery, as the sherd will be imprinted with lines from the brush.

Change the water regularly. On some sites this may be difficult, but dirty water may leave smear marks necessitating the rewashing of the piece, which will not be good for it.

With very fragile pieces use small swabs of cotton wool moistened with water. If necessary pad the washing bowl with a towel in case the object or part of the object falls.

Drying

Most finds can be air dried. However, never leave them to dry in direct sunlight or near a heat source. Heat causes materials to expand. This may cause cracking, particularly in materials such as ivory, and in glazed pottery where the glaze may become detached. On the other hand, do not keep them in a damp environment as this can encourage mould to grow. If an item has a lid or stopper do not leave it to dry with the lid on as this will cause condensation.

Wet Storage

Organic materials such as leather or wood, which have been recovered wet and need to be kept wet, should be stored in strong polythene bags. Place the object(s) in one bag and cover with cool, clean water. Do not drown the item or fill the bag so much that it is too heavy to lift. Do not add fungicides or any other chemicals (despite advice in various books) as fungicide may interfere with any carbon-14 dating. It may also form uneven deposits on the leather after freeze-drying. Also, amounts are difficult to estimate and if too much is used this may pose a hazard not only to those processing the leather but also to those who work on leather at a later date, such as the conservators.

Place the first bag inside a second one in case the first becomes punctured. Secure the bags with staples but make sure the water does not come in contact with the staples as these will rust and may stain the artefact. This is another reason why the bags should not contain too much water. Store the bags in as dark an area as possible. Plastic bins can be used for this and the lack of light will prevent the growth of mould, which needs light to grow.

Check the bags regularly, particularly throughout hot seasons, as the water will evaporate. If the finds are allowed to dry out they may crack and, in extreme cases, disintegrate.

Dry Storage

Ensure the piece is completely dry before packing: if it is not, condensation may form, which will encourage the growth of mould.

Fragile pieces should be supported with acid-free tissue paper and if necessary put into a polystyrene (crystal) box – obtainable from conservators – and again supported with acid-free tissue paper.

Chapter 1
MATERIALS

In order to be able to identify artefacts it is important that the finder can first identify the materials they are made of. For example, ivory, bone and antler can be notoriously difficult to distinguish when found separately, and this can have detrimental results, particularly in relation to washing, drying and storing. The guidelines given here are intended as outlines only, but they should be sufficient to enable the identification of the materials mentioned in this book.

Soils

All soils in Britain are regarded as damp but contain different amounts and types of minerals, chemicals, oxygen and moisture. The most damaging conditions are created by those soils high in oxygen and moisture. In conditions where oxygen levels are low, such as waterlogged ground, or without moisture, such as dry environments, survival can be reasonably good. Organic materials will survive quite well in anaerobic conditions such as in waterlogged soil, where there is little or no oxygen, and other conditions such as damp clay which is also low in oxygen. Soils are described, broadly, as being alkaline, acidic or neutral. Neutral is the best soil for preservation. The tables at the end of the discussion of each material are for guidance only. Soil conditions vary from site to site and will therefore produce individual differences of survival.

Metals

Today there are eighty-six known metals. However, until the late thirteenth century there were only seven and these are generally referred to as the Metals of Antiquity. One of the reasons for this is that, although not all common, they do occur in many locations throughout the world so were available to most ancient civilisations. The seven are: gold, copper, silver, lead, tin, iron and mercury. Of the seven, five are found in a natural state: gold, silver, copper, iron (from meteors) and mercury. (Mercury is not covered in this book as artefacts were not made from it).

In the thirteenth and fourteenth centuries, arsenic, antimony, zinc and bismuth were discovered. Platinum was discovered in the sixteenth century and nickel in 1751.

Gold (Au)

Gold is the earliest metal known to humans and one of the seven Metals of Antiquity. It would initially have been recovered from alluvial finds, either from streams or eroded deposits, and would have been hammered to weld it together. As early as the Iron Age in Britain gold was being mined rather than collected, and the mine of Dolaucothi, South Wales, dates to this period.

Gold, even in its natural form, is rarely pure and is often alloyed with silver (referred to as electrum). Generally gold is far too soft to be of much practical use so it is deliberately alloyed with other metals (particularly silver and copper) to provide strength. Even so, it remains a very malleable metal and can be made into extremely thin sheets, such as gold leaf, a type of tissue paper to be used for gilding on other materials. It is also very ductile, so is easy to work and can be hammered into shape or cast into moulds. It can be drawn into a wire as fine as to be almost invisible to the human eye and resists acids (why it is used in teeth) and therefore will not taint food and drink. Much of the gold recovered has been used in jewellery and coins, but one third of all the gold ever found is held in government reserves.

The colour of gold can vary according to the metal it has been alloyed with. If there is a reasonable amount of silver present then the gold will appear an amber colour. If there is a large silver content then the gold may appear almost white (not to be confused with 'white gold' which is an alloy of platinum). When copper is present the gold may appear a reddish colour.

Survival

Gold is an inert metal and therefore very stable. It is resistant to acids so does not corrode or tarnish. Gold recovered from deposits thousands of years old can appear as fresh as if it had been bought yesterday. However, gold that is heavily alloyed with other metals, particularly silver and copper, may corrode; the corrosion properties will take on the characteristics of the other metal. Therefore, heavily alloyed gold should be dealt with as either silver or copper.

Gold can occasionally be confused with waterlogged copper, which may appear similar in appearance. However, waterlogged copper is slightly duller than gold.

Care

Gold can be cleaned in tepid water with a cloth. However, beware of composite items particularly if they include enamelling or niello which can be rubbed off easily.

Gold Survival

Alkaline soils	Neutral soils	Acidic soils
Y	Y	Y
Waterlogged alkaline soils	Waterlogged neutral soils	Waterlogged acidic soils
Y	Y	Y

Copper (Cu)

Copper is the oldest smelted metal in the world and its use dates back some 10,000 years. Native copper is found in Britain mainly in Cornwall (in the eighteenth and nineteenth centuries more than half world's output came from Cornwall), the Lake District (the first large-scale production in Britain was at Keswick) and North Wales, but in antiquity most copper was obtained from smelting ores. It is a very malleable and ductile metal and can be hammered into shape. It has a high melting point of 1086°C but in order for it to be molten enough to pour it has to be heated to 1300°C. If breaks occur during hammering, the metal is simply heated up or 'annealed' to continue. As pure copper is softer than quartz a copper knife would not be sharper than a flint blade so flints were still produced after copper came into use. The advantage of a copper blade is that it can be resharpened indefinitely whereas flint can only be reused a finite number of times. Prehistoric metal axes were cast and the cutting edge was finished by hammering (see Bronze Axes, pages 170). Hammering not only increased the hardness of the blade but allowed it to be quite thin, compared to the cutting edge of a flint axe.

From the twelfth to the fifteenth centuries, pure copper was often used for ecclesiastical objects such as pyxes, reliquaries and crosiers, mainly because the softer nature of the material made it easier to apply enamel and gilding to it than to bronze or brass.

Until the eighteenth century and mechanisation, copper items were often made from several sheets, so the surface will appear slightly uneven with hand-hammering marks and joins visible. Modern copper items are usually made from one sheet and have a uniform thickness. On pre-industrial vessels the bases of copper items will often be thicker than the rest, to protect against wear and as a heat insulator. Modern examples do not have this.

Copper has a high electrical and thermal conductivity; it conducts an electrical current better than any other metal except silver. It has always been used in industry for pipes and wiring. Other uses are for roofs – the familiar green appearance of many buildings implies a copper (or copper-alloy)-clad roof. Perhaps the best-known use of copper is in the Statue of Liberty .

Copper in itself is often too soft for many practical purposes, so it is alloyed with various other metals to enhance its strength. In the current industrial market there are over 400 recognised copper-based alloys. However, in archaeological records the three main copper alloys are those considered here: bronze, brass and latten. It should be noted that without the aid of magnification it is too difficult to distinguish between bronze and brass so for recording purposes both are usually referred to as 'copper-alloy'.

Survival

Copper items will appear different according to their burial conditions.

Dark green: The most common colour of recovered copper. With a slow rate of corrosion the surface colour may be a dark green with the form and details of the artefact showing up well. If corrosion is rapid, the green surface layer may be thick and the form and details of the object difficult to make out, or in extreme conditions they may be completely lost.

White/grey: Rich with lead or tin alloys.

Black and shiny: Most often from waterlogged conditions where sulphides are present.

Bright yellow with pitted surface: From waterlogged conditions and often mistaken for gold.

Care

Do not wash copper objects, as this will accelerate the corrosion process. A soft brush may be used to clean surface dirt but if the metal is in a very powdery condition or has 'bronze disease' do not attempt any cleaning.

Copper was often added to make composite items so beware when cleaning artefacts that the copper parts are not made wet.

	Copper Survival	
Alkaline soils	Neutral soils	Acidic soils
Y	Y	N
Waterlogged alkaline soils	Waterlogged neutral soils	Waterlogged acidic soils
Y	Y	N

Bronze

During prehistoric times there was a broad range of copper alloys being produced, particularly in areas where tin was not readily available. The normal definition of bronze is copper alloyed with tin, but other metals could be added such as lead or arsenic which made the bronze harder. Tin not only lowers the melting point but makes the bronze harder and less malleable. The optimum alloy, 10-12 per cent tin, has great fluidity as it lowers the melting point by 100°C, and, with only a slight contraction when cooled, it makes bronze especially suited to being cast into moulds. It also holds the form of the mould very well and can be hammered and annealed to become stronger. The casting process of bronze went through three stages. First, the bronze was cast into a mould of sand, clay or stone until the mould was full; later, it was cast around an iron core, probably in order to save on bronze and the later still it was cast around a clay core thereby producing an outline of the core.

During the Bronze Age, harder metal began to be used regularly for tools and weapons, among other things. It polishes well and was often used for mirrors. As it can withstand heat well it was also popular for cooking items.

Bronze colours vary according to the alloy. It also darkens with age and the newer the bronze, the lighter the colour. If rich in tin it may have a corrosion patina of a greyish colour. If more than 30 per cent tin, with a distinct grey/white appearance and hard, the metal is called speculum. This is more brittle but can take a high polish and so was used for mirrors.

Survival

Dark green: A slow corrosion: the form and decoration are usually well preserved.

Light green and powdery: If the conditions are particularly bad the surface may be light green and powdery, with dark green spots and may flake easily. Below the green layer there may be a red-brown layer. Signs of intense corrosion may include hard warts and blisters with pitting over the artefact. The pits are areas where the corrosion has been faster than in other areas. If the powdery corrosion is underneath the surface and in the pits the artefact will probably have what is called 'bronze disease'. The form of the artefact and surface details will be difficult to make out and the object will be fragile.

Gold coloured: Waterlogged bronze may appear bright in colour and shiny and in these circumstances can be mistaken for gold. In contexts where oxygen is scarce the bronze may appear black.

Bronze disease

Care

Do not wet but use a soft brush to remove corrosion deposits. If recovered wet allow to air dry and then brush.

Bronze Survival

Alkaline soils	Neutral soils	Acidic soils
Y	Y	Y
Waterlogged alkaline soils	Waterlogged neutral soils	Waterlogged acidic soils
Y	Y	Y

Brass

Brass is an alloy of copper and zinc although most zinc inclusions were from smelted ores. Some brass contains or tin, which has a greater anti-corrosive property. Brass is found in Iron Age and Roman contexts with some Roman coins being made from brass, as well as some military equipment and jewellery. In medieval times brass was used for monument brass panels in church floors to commemorate the dead. During Tudor times brass wire and pins were produced but it was not until the sixteenth–seventeenth centuries when pure zinc was imported from Asia that brass became popular. European zinc production started in the eighteenth century, and prior to that it had been extracted from the ore calamine (particularly found in the Mendip Hills, Somerset, from the late sixteenth century onwards), from which it is difficult to extract zinc. Due to its ease of manufacture and corrosion-resistant properties, brass was utilised for many items.

Brass is impossible to distinguish from bronze without a microscope and so both are generally referred to as copper alloys. However, generally brass is less durable and less delicate than bronze.

The colour of brass depends on the quantity of zinc present, and age varies the colour in different ways. With small amounts of zinc the brass will be a reddish colour and soft. A medium amount and the brass will be yellow-golden and will be soft enough to press into moulds; in this way it was often used for military buttons. With large amounts, although the brass will be harder, it is less malleable and cannot be press-moulded. Very high amounts of zinc make the brass too brittle for use. The greater the amount of zinc, the paler the colour will be. Other metals such as tin or aluminium may be added to brass; these add an anti-corrosive property.

Early brass was hand-hammered, which leaves an uneven thickness. With industrialisation brass was produced by machines and so became thinner and more even. It was also much cheaper than bronze.

Survival
Brass survives well.

Care
Do not wet but use a soft brush to remove corrosion deposits. If recovered wet allow to air dry and then brush.

	Brass Survival	
Alkaline soils	Neutral soils	Acidic soils
Y	Y	Y
Waterlogged alkaline soils	Waterlogged neutral soils	Waterlogged acidic soils
Y	Y	Y

Latten

Latten is a term that was used in the fourteenth–eighteenth centuries for a zinc–copper alloy valued for its corrosion resistance but which today would be referred to as brass. There are three forms of latten: black latten which is usually unpolished; shaven latten which is generally very thin, and roll latten which, unlike the first two, is polished on both sides. The best quality has a golden colour which indicates high zinc levels. In the medieval period latten was imported but was often diluted to make it cheaper, so it lacks the golden colour. When calamine, from which zinc is founded, was found in the Mendips a latten industry began there.

Latten was used for a wide range of items and was generally made in thin sheets hammered into shape. It was used especially for monumental brasses and effigies. The screen of Henry VII's tomb in Westminster Abbey contains some good examples. Many church utensils such as candlesticks, crosses, etc. were made of latten, as were other items such as purse bars, spurs and spoons; these objects were not, as is popularly thought, made of bronze.

Survival

Latten survives well.

Care

As brass.

Silver (Ag)

One of the Metals of Antiquity, silver occurs naturally and within simple ores such as electrum and galena from which the metal is extracted. Like other precious metals it is fairly uncommon and in particular silver as a commodity in Europe was quite rare, until it was mined regularly in the New World (1500–1875).

Silver's popularity is partly due to its shine and bright colour, but it tarnishes easily, particularly when in association with sulphur, a common pollutant assocaiated with fossil fuels. It is harder than gold but softer than copper; is malleable and ductile and has been made into numerous items (the most common silver finds are coins). To make silver stronger it is often alloyed with other metals, particularly copper, and generally the more copper present the duller the silver appears; thus, the brighter the metal the purer the silver. Sterling silver is 92.5 per cent silver and 7.5 per cent copper and is hallmarked with the lion passant (see page 167 for silver hallmarks).

Survival

Silver survives reasonably well in soils but will corrode rapidly in anaerobic conditions where salt is present; it is particularly vulnerable in seawater. In soils that contain high levels of chloride ions a protective grey-brown layerof silver chloride may form on the surface of silver. If there are traces of green this may well indicate that copper corrosion has occurred (see page 19) and when dealing with silver items that contain a high percentage of copper it may be advisable to treat them as copper. If recovered from a damp environment the silver may initially appear a dull grey/white but turn to a lilac colour when exposed to the atmosphere. The most common appearance, however, is for silver to appear quite black, or purple/black and smooth. If the object has corroded extensively the form may be seen by x-raying it.

Care

Do not wet silver when recovered dry but allow it to air dry.

Never use a hard brush such as a toothbrush on a silver item as, being relatively soft, it will be easily scratched. Ideally a silver item should be removed quickly to a conservator as the corrosion may be accelerated by the contact with the atmosphere. Sulphur is constantly present in the atmosphere due to the burning of fossil fuels. It also enters the atmosphere through the rubbing or erosion of carpets, paints and wood. This is why, when silver is stored in wooden cabinets, tarnish may still affect the pieces. It should therefore be stored with compatible materials such as china and glass. Plastics and fabrics will encourage tarnish. Do not store silver in anything other than recommended archival tissue paper and cardboard boxes. If there is a large quantity of silver recovered and conservation or specialist attention is not immediately available the purchase of 'silvercloth' which is generally available is recommended for storage. Oily deposits from fingers will leave deposits which will tarnish: therefore avoid handling silver as much as possible and instead use a buffer such as acid-free tissue paper. If necessary acquire cotton or latex gloves from a museum or conservator. Rubber gloves are not recommended as they emit gaseous sulphur compounds (SO_2).

A black tarnish layer is difficult to remove on silver. Traditionally the removal of the black is done by cleaning with a commercial abrasive, many of which can be bought in the shops. However, great care needs to be practised when buying and using these. Cheap versions may be too abrasive and too heavy-handed cleaning may cause the abrasive gradually to remove the surface of the silver. In old silver that has been repeatedly cleaned the item can be quite thin and any decoration may appear faint.

Silver Survival

Alkaline soils	Neutral soils	Acidic soils
Y	Y	Y
Waterlogged alkaline soils	Waterlogged neutral soils	Waterlogged acidic soils
Y	Y	Y

Lead (Pb)

Lead is a very heavy, soft, grey metal that is easily malleable. It can be easily broken, especially if bent several times in one spot. It has a melting point of 327°C so can be heated in a domestic fire and cast into moulds. Lead does not exist in its pure form but is extracted from a variety of minerals, the prime one being galena, lead sulphide (PbS), anglesite, cerrusite and mimim. In its original state lead is a silvery blue metal of bright lustre but changes to a dull grey when exposed to air. Lead can be toughened by adding a small amount of antimony or other metals to it.

Lead is one of the oldest metals in use (probably around 7,000 years) because the minerals from which it is extracted are widespread and it is easy to extract. It was mined in quantity during the Roman period from the Mendips in Somerset and on Greenhow Hill, Yorkshire. Ingots (or 'pigs') of lead from Yorkshire and Derbyshire have also been found with the stamp *EX ARG* meaning 'from the silver mines'. A number of ingots of Roman lead, some bearing inscriptions, have been found. Lead was cast into these ingots for transport and made into objects by those who purchased them. Lead was used extensively for many items, from lining vessels that store water and wine, to glazes on ceramics (see lead glaze, page 126). It was also used for containers to hold highly corrosive liquids, as it is relatively resistant to corrosion. Lead is extremely resistant to weather, not being affected by the rain or frost, and so was used in plumbing, as leaded windows, loom weights or net-sinkers. As it can be hammered with a low heat, sheet lead was cheaply produced and was used for roofing. Many churches' roofs and spires were covered with lead. It was also commonly used for coffins from Roman times onwards and the Romans would often cast them with patterns in relief, as can be seen on the coffin from Spitalfields, London.

After the Romans left Britain (fifth century), lead mining declined and did not recover until the twelfth century. At this time lead production was mainly in the hands of the Church. Production suffered again, as with most other industries, at the time of the Black Death (late four-teenth–early fifteenth century); it then recovered, but suf-fered a further setback during the Dissolution of the Monasteries (1536–1540) when lead removed from the monasteries flooded the market. During the seventeenth and eighteenth centuries, the north of England was a major production area for lead and the landscape still shows evidence of the spoil heaps. Lead production fol-lowed a steady course until the nineteenth century, which saw a golden age for all British metals when Britain became the leading metal producer of the world. Most lead mining ceased between 1880 and 1900.

Baptismal fonts were often made of lead, between the eleventh and fourteenth centuries, and it was used in bul-lets, shot, solder and pewter. The castles and cathedrals of Europe contain considerable quantities of lead in decora-tive fixtures, roofs, pipes and windows.

Survival

Lead corrodes rapidly so many items from antiquity will have been lost. It was also often resmelted. Its corrosion properties are very similar to tin and pewter.

White, white-brown, pale brown, white-grey coating: This is the most common appearance of corrosion. Some artefacts may have a surface covering of soil mixed with the corro-sion.

Dark grey/black layer: The usual signs from waterlogged conditions.

Light grey patches and dark grey warts: Will also have a fri-able surface.

Lead is toxic in large amounts and after long exposure, so if an extensive quantity of lead is being excavated, health and safety procedures must be followed.

Care

Do not wet but use a soft brush to remove corrosion deposits. If recovered wet allow to air dry and then brush.

Lead Survival

Alkaline Soils	Neutral soils	Acidic soils
Y	Y	N
Waterlogged alkaline soils	Waterlogged neutral soils	Waterlogged acidic soils
Y	Y	N

Tin (Sn)

Tin is a silvery, malleable and ductile metal that is reasonably corrosion resistant if it is looked after. However, it becomes brittle when subject to heat. Pure tin is rare, rarer than zinc, copper and lead, and the metal is mainly recovered from the mineral cassiterite, or tin dioxide. Cornwall has seen a thriving tin trade from antiquity to the last century, but now over 35 countries mine tin.

Tin on its own is difficult to cast and too weak and brittle to be used for items other than small objects (when tin is bent it gives out its famous 'tin cry', a kind of high scraping sound made by the internal crystals breaking). Due to its hardening effect on copper, tin was used in bronze implements as early as 3500 BC and its ability to bond with other metals meant it was often used to coat them to prevent corrosion. Additionally, it can be highly polished to resemble silver (although its colour dulls over time) and tin-plating was regarded as the poor person's silver. Tin is resistant to organic acids and so was often used to coat copper-alloy vessels, particularly cooking and serving vessels and utensils. The remains of a tin coating can often be seen in corners and underneath vessels. Today we are most familiar with tin as tin-plated steel used as containers for food preservation.

In the late sixteenth–early seventeenth centuries tin-plated objects became popular. These were formed by dipping sheets of iron in a bath of molten tin. They were then usually hammered over a former so hammer marks are often quite visible. Pontypool, South Wales, became famous for its tin-plated ware; it was regarded as superior even to the

German product where the technique originated. In 1728 a technique for producing sheet tin in rolling mills was invented and a wide range of objects were made from tinned iron. On these, hammer marks are less obvious though joins from the sheets may be seen.

Survival

Tin does not survive well in the soil. An alloy recovered that has a high tin content may have a smooth surface or some ugly warts. Sometimes there are deep cracks. The colour of corrosion ranges from black to grey-brown to white. It may be brittle when recovered.

Care

Avoid getting tin wet but allow to air dry if it is already wet. It can then be stored normally in plastic bags, but make sure the bag is perforated to avoid condensation forming.

	Tin Survival	
Alkaline soils	Neutral soils	Acidic soils
Y	Y	N
Waterlogged alkaline soils	Waterlogged neutral soils	Waterlogged acidic soils
Y	Y	N

Pewter

The composition of pewter varies depending on the age of manufacture, but the main constituent is tin, with varying amounts of lead, copper, antimony (introduced in the late seventeenth century) and bismuth. The most controversial constituent, due to its toxicity, is lead and strict rules were laid down in medieval times to control the amount included. Roman pewter, however, used large quantities of lead (from 50–90 per cent) with the most common alloy being 60–80 per cent lead to 40–20 per cent tin, an alloy also used in early medieval times. Pewter softens when worked so it does not need to be annealed (heated repeatedly) and can be hammered from sheet metal. As pewter is a soft metal with a low melting point, it could not be used for cooking items. Its softness also meant it had a relatively short life, added to which it is a recyclable metal so damaged objects were traded as part payment and melted down. Most pewter is cast: spoons would be cast in two-part moulds, but larger items such as flagons would be cast in multi-part moulds. It is then hammered to compact and strengthen it. When new, pewter is a bright, silver colour (another 'poor person's silver') but unless it is polished regularly it quickly acquires a patina of oxidation which produces the dull grey colour that today is most commonly associated with pewter. Differences in pewter alloys are often associated with wealth. High-grade pewter, known as hard or plate pewter contained copper and was lead-free. Cheaper pewter was high in lead and these items are subject to distortion due to the ability of lead to bend easily. For almost 500 years pewter was one of the most important metals in a domestic context, used frequently for flatware such as plates and saucers as well as spoons (see page 161), tankards, candlesticks, etc.

Roman pewter first appeared in the mid-third century AD, and finds have been made in Lincolnshire, Gloucestershire and Suffolk consisting of plates, vases, bowls and flagons. Pewter was also used for seals of office and other small items. It was generally cast in moulds and then trimmed on a lathe and used for a wide range of wares particularly during the third–fifth centuries. Pewter then fell out of use until the eleventh century when the first recorded use, in 1076, is in the churches when silver could not be afforded. Its use then rose steadily over the centuries until the fourteenth, when pewter was used throughout Europe as the material of the common people replacing wood, horn and pottery. Until the beginning of the fourteenth century, items were rarely marked. However, throughout Europe guilds were being formed and in 1348 an established standard alloy was introduced.

Until 1550 most items were utilitarian and neither artistic nor decorative. However, after this time there was a move away from traditional designs, and the period 1666-1705 is regarded as the golden age of pewter. In 1503 it became obligatory to include a maker's mark. By the early seventeenth century the range of pewter items was wider; they were made in greater quantities and enormous amounts were shipped aboard. Antimony was introduced in the late seventeenth century in order to keep down the lead content. Despite the growing quantity and range of pewter, many of the shapes kept to traditional forms and there was never a great variety in design as moulds were expensive to produce. It was never greatly decorated because of its softness, except for a period of design between 1660 and 1720 called 'wriggle-work', which is a fine engraving with a narrow, chisel-like tool rocked back and forth to form zig-zag patterns.

Wriggle-work

Britannia Metal

In the late eighteenth century, Britannia metal, an alloy of 90 per cent tin and 10 per cent antimony, although often with small amounts of lead, copper or bismuth, was introduced. Britannia metal has caused controversy, with many questions about its designation as 'pewter'. However as its main alloy is tin it is little different from the other kinds of pewter. It was used not only as a replacement for pewter but also as a base for silver-plated items. It is essentially similar to pewter, the difference being in the method of manufacture. Britannia metal was spun, stamped or rolled with the result that a harder alloy was produced, which was therefore more practical, and items are also lighter and thinner. It could be coloured by the addition of copper, producing a yellow tint. Britannia metal was used for the same traditional wares as pewter and was common in coffee and tea pots. Much of it was made in Birmingham and Sheffield; Victorian Britannia metal pieces were often electroplated with silver, and stamped EPBM. Without constant attention Britannia metal quickly looses its silvery sheen.

By the late eighteenth century the growing popularity and cheapness of the brighter, more colourful porcelain and fine earthenware meant that pewter was replaced in many domestic utensils and by the Victorian Age pewter use had been reduced to pubs only. However, by 1930 pubs were banned from using pewter tankards unless specifically asked for by customers. In the early twentieth century pewter underwent a revival during the Art Nouveau period. Today pewter alloy is 94 per cent tin, 4 per cent antimony and 2 per cent copper or bismuth as set by the British Standards Institution in 1969.

Maker's Marks

In 1474 maker's marks indicating the quality of the pewter were introduced and generally consist of initials within a cartouche. However, it was not until 1503 that makers were officially required to mark their pieces with touch marks in an attempt to control the amount of poisonous lead being used in pewter. Nearly all sixteenth-century spoons bear a touch mark (see page 162), the early ones consisting simply of two initials within a circle or oval cartouche. Spoons are the most common type of pewter recovered from the sixteenth century as they were so easily lost. The maker's mark was stamped on, never engraved. They appear mainly on the handle of a mug, or on the rim of a plate. Later, the marks got larger and moved to the base of the piece.

In the seventeenth century, the touch marks came to include full names for the first time, and were generally more ornate.

Rose and Crown

In 1543 it became obligatory to use a Tudor rosette, originally as a sign for export, but it quickly came to be regarded, not only in Britain but in Europe, as a guarantee of very high-quality pewter. The Tudor rose was maintained by Europe as it was using a lot of British tin. The rose became crowned in around 1566 and initials under the crown are those of the maker.

Town Mark

Town marks were also used and these generally take several forms, such as a coat of arms, heraldic device or seal of town or city, and the name of the town. Town marks were made redundant in the eighteenth century when maker's marks included the name of the town. In the 1870s, a town number was added.

Year Mark

A year mark may be included but this refers to when the maker opened the shop and not the year of manufacture. In some cases it may be used by families as an 'established in…' date.

'Hallmarks'

From 1635 'hallmarks' appeared in an attempt to imitate those on silver, despite repeated complaints from the Goldsmith's Company. As these are not proper hallmarks (see page 167) they are referred to here in inverted commas. They are usually set four in a line, in black lettering (see page 201) with one or more of a lion passant, leopard's head, Britannia, lion rampant, harp, thistle, buckle or anchor. As with other marks, the use of 'hallmarks' spread to the Continent. By 1680 they had increased in size; they then remained consistent until the nineteenth century when lines of three or five 'hallmarks' were also used.

X Mark

From 1694 to the eighteenth century, items of exceptionally high quality were marked with an X, sometimes crowned.

London Mark

The word 'London' was used from the seventeenth century but was quickly adopted by the rest of the country as a mark of quality and is not a location mark.

Superfine Hard Metal

In the eighteenth century the words 'superfine hard metal' commonly appeared on pewter wares, indicating no lead content and a high quality pewter.

Capacity Marks

Prior to 1826 a common mark that was applied by the pewterer was a crowned WR mark, usually intended to signify that the measure reached the William III ale standard. However, in 1826 official Imperial Standards marks were introduced on vessels that were used to measure liquids – for example drinking or measuring cups. Until 1878 these marks varied in style from town to town but were standardised in that year as a crown over the initials of the reigning monarch (see below), often within an oval and including a town number. They may also include the word 'Imperial' or a heraldic borough and/or county stamp:

AR below a crown: Queen Anne
WR below a crown: William III
WIV below a crown: William IV
GIV below a crown: George IV
VR below a crown: Victoria

Survival

Pewter corrosion is similar to that of lead and tin and the extent of the corrosion will depend on the composition of the alloy. Objects with a high lead content will be susceptible to corrosion, of which the most common appearance is a surface layer of brown soil mixed with a white powdery residue. Below this the surface has a white to grey surface coating. Look for white powdery spots which will indicate active corrosion: if present, do not attempt to treat it but refer to a conservator. Damp and cold can seriously affect pewter, so much so that corrosion can occur to the point where holes will appear in the metal. Different colours may be visible due to the different alloys but may also result from the artefact's surroundings; for example, a pub tankard that has spent a long time in a smoky atmosphere may take on a brown tinge.

Care

Objects with a high lead content are often distorted when recovered. Do not attempt to manipulate the piece in any way as any stresses may cause it to break, particularly as pewter has a tendency to be brittle on recovery. It may also show signs of lamination and have an uneven surface.

When cleaning use only a soft brush as due to the softness of the metal it is easily scratched. The dull grey oxide film that coats most pewter is a protective layer and no attempt should ever be made to remove it.

Pewter Survival

Alkaline soils	Neutral soils	Acidic soils
N	Y	N
Waterlogged alkaline soils	Waterlogged neutral soils	Waterlogged acidic soils
N	Y	N

Iron (Fe)

Iron was discovered in around 1000 BC but it was not used widely until the fifth century BC.

Iron ores are widespread and abundant and many of them were used in antiquity. The purest iron ores are magnetite (approximately 72 per cent iron) and haematite (approximately 69 per cent iron). It is softer than quartz but harder than copper or the copper alloys, and came to replace most of the copper-alloy tools, despite requiring a more laborious method of production. It can be fair to say that iron revolutionised both weapons and farming. Iron has the highest melting point of all prehistoric metals – 1,500°C – and is more difficult to purify than other metals. It is extremely malleable and a very sharp edge can be achieved. In most periods iron was always reused.

In prehistoric times the only way that iron could be manipulated to make artefacts was by hammering and drawing. It can be hammered paper-thin and the more it is hammered, drawn out and annealed the stronger and tougher it becomes. This meant that moulds were no longer needed and it could be used to make large items where strength but lightness was required.

With the addition of a small quantity of carbon, iron can be converted into steel which, although less strong, has a hard quality that makes it suitable for items such as knives.

Cast iron has its origins in the sixteenth century but its widespread use is mainly modern. It is not suited to fine work.

Survival

Iron can corrode very quickly and when recovered in a corroded state can take on a variety of appearances. If in doubt use a magnet, for if enough of the original metal is left it will give a positive response. Bear in mind that even if a response is not forthcoming it may still be iron but much of the metal may have deteriorated.

Orange-brown colour: Rust of this colour will appear most commonly on the outermost layers when the item has been recovered from an aerobic (oxygen-rich) context. It may be very thick and the form of the original item may not be obvious, it may also be encrusted with grit and small stones. If exposed to a great deal of oxygen it may appear bright orange with protuberances and be light in weight. If compared weight for weight with a similar item it may be possible to gain an idea of how much of the original item has been lost.

Underneath the orange-brown layers a dark, grey-black layer may be apparent, which can indicate that the original shape may still be intact. Or it may be that only an outer layer exists and the internal core has become hollow. Bright orange powdery areas show proof of active corrosion and this must be arrested as soon as possible.

White to light grey coating: This may be apparent when the iron has been buried in chalk soils. The metal may only be lightly corroded and retain much of the original shape.

Black, or golden, even texture: Most probably comes from waterlogged conditions where oxygen is low or not present. It may appear with additional blue patches. Corrosion will differ according to the structure of the item; if it is thin, or parts (such as handles) protrude, these may corrode more quickly than other thicker areas.

Blue: From phosphate (i.e. high nitrate) conditons.

Care

Do not wash iron objects as this will accelerate the corrosion process. Do not place in direct sunlight, near a radiator or subject to direct heat (e.g. from a heater) as this will dry the item out too quickly and it may begin to flake. Take care when washing composite items and try not to wet those parts which include iron, such as iron rivets. Also watch for pieces of organics attached to iron pieces, such as textiles adhering to a rivet. If in doubt about conserving a number of materials in one piece, contact a conservator. Many small pieces such as nails can be dried at room temperature and packaged in bags. However, for more important items place in a polythene box, such as a Tupperware box, with a silica gel sachet. The silica gel will absorb the moisture, allowing the item to dry out in a controlled environment. Once the silica gel is saturated must be replaced. With the old types of silica gel, when it is dark blue it is dry, and when damp it will turn pink. However, these types of silica gel are now considered harmful and are not recommended.

Initial water absorption of the gel may be high and so it is important to monitor it. Once the box is sealed it should be opened as little as possible, as opening the box will subject the silica gel to moisture from the outside and it may become saturated more quickly. To this end a humidity indicator should be placed against the inside of the box facing outwards so that it may be read without opening the box.

Another means of testing whether the piece is dry is to weigh it regularly: when there is no further weight loss it is dry.

If, however, iron items have been recovered from water-logged conditions, keep them wet and consult a conservator.

Iron Survival

Alkaline soils	Neutral soils	Acidic soils
Y	Y	N
Waterlogged alkaline soils	Waterlogged neutral soils	Waterlogged acidic soils
Y	Y	N

Steel

Steel is an alloy of iron and there are many different kinds available. However, carbon steel is the most common and widely used. With an increase of carbon in the firing process, the steel is harder and has a higher tensile strength than iron, but it is more brittle. It is less susceptible to rust and corrosion than iron. Steel can be hammered or annealed although when annealing steel it must be allowed to cool very slowly. During most of its existence steel was expensive to produce and was therefore reserved for those items needing extra strength, such as cutting implements. Early steel was used in a small strip on knife blades as it was cheaper than making the entire blade of steel and could be replaced more cheaply (see page 157). The most famous steel in antiquity was Damascus steel, a complicated alloy with a number of different materials. In 1889 steel was introduced as a building material at the World Expo in Paris with the construction of the Eiffel Tower.

Steel is not that easy to distinguish from iron as the colour is very similar, but it has a lighter note when struck.

Stainless steel is a modern alloy of iron with chromium and vanadium and has more than 60 different grades. The chromium is the ingredient that gives stainless steel its unique corrosion-resistant properties. Steel is favoured in culinary implements as it does not taint food.

Survival

Steel survives fairly well in most conditions.

Cleaning

Do not wet steel, but allow to air dry and then package as normal.

Steel Survival

Alkaline soils	Neutral soils	Acidic soils
Y	Y	N
Waterlogged alkaline soils	Waterlogged neutral soils	Waterlogged acidic soils
Y	Y	N

Inorganics
Glass

The earliest use of glass dates to the third millennium BC in Mesopotamia, when it was being used mainly as glazes on ceramic vessels. 'Glass', like 'ceramic', is a broad term which covers materials such as glazes (a vitreous coating applied to another material), enamels (glazes applied to metals) and faience. It is referred to as a super-cooled liquid as it has the characteristics of both solid and liquid.

Glass also comes in varieties; it can be a natural green colour which occurs when no colourants have been added; it may be coloured by the addition of metallic oxides; it can occur as lead glass, a clear glass that can be easily etched; it can be free-form blown or blown into moulds; floated to make sheet glass, or moulded. It can be decorated either in its molten or solid state and can range from the utilitarian to the extremely ornate.

Evidence for early glassworking in Britain has increased significantly in the last few decades as familiarity grows with the types of artefacts needed to securely identify glass manufacturing/working sites. When faience beads were found at British Bronze Age sites the original belief was that they were imported, possibly from Egypt. It is now known that they were made in Britain and over 250 Bronze Age beads have come from over 15 areas, including sites in Scotland. During the Iron Age the use of coloured enamel glass to decorate high-quality goods increases, as can be seen from noted examples such as the Battersea Shield and the Witham Shield. Some of the largest accumulations of beads from the Iron Age have been found at the workshops at the East and West Lake villages of Meare, Somerset, and date from the fourth to second centuries BC. Blue glass is the most common colour in Iron Age Europe: the cobalt needed for this colour came mainly from Germany, Austria, Switzerland and Czechoslovakia and this use of imports may suggest complex trade routes.

Glass blowing began in late first century BC in Syria and both the method and the long hollow iron tube (about 1.2m) used for blowing have changed little since then. The Romans adopted this method but improved it by blowing glass into moulds to increase the variety of shapes. The Romans were also the first to use glass for windows in the first century AD, although it was a green colour and opaque, so visibility would have been limited. Window glass is a common find on Roman sites. The pieces are generally flat, natural green-blue with a rough side where the glass was laid to dry. They tend not to be of uniform thickness and so distort the view through the pane; they were intended mainly to let in light. However, to overcome this defect the pane could be ground and polished.

Bottles were used, mainly in the first and second centuries AD, for the transportation and storage of liquids. Small fragments are often identifiable as being from bottles by fine scratches on the outer surface, caused by the basket holders that the bottles were placed in. There is no contemporary literary evidence to support glass production in Britain but archaeological evidence has been found. Some of the most overlooked pieces of evidence are moiles. These are small pieces broken from the end of a blowing-iron or detached from a blown vessel and definitely indicate the practice of glass blowing. However, they are relatively rare, as normally they would have been added to the cullet to be reused. Because they are hard to recognise, there is the question of how much has not yet been identified, or kept.

Once the Romans had departed from Britain window panes were usually made of horn and until the late medieval period, the only window glass would have been found in luxurious buildings and churches. It was during the medieval period that stained glass windows reached peak in design.

Around AD 1000, significant changes took place in glass production. Until this time soda glass was the main glass in use. Due to difficulties in importing the main ingredient, natron (sodium carbonate), potash (potassium caarbonate) glass took over as potash could be obtained much more cheaply, being made from burning vegetation, including wood, and from sands. Small amounts of common salt and manganese are added to make the glass clear but even so it is still less clear than soda glass. Potash glass was more common in Europe. Until 1700 Venetian glass dominated the European market.

In 1673 the English glassmaker George Ravenscroft (1618-1681) added lead oxide to potash glass. This resulted in a brilliant glass with a high refractive index, so it was ideal for lenses, prisms and imitation jewels. In recent times it has been used for shields in nuclear installations. It was also a heavy glass but the addition of lead made it soft enough for etching. English lead glass came to be considered the finest glass of the eighteenth century and dominated European and colonial markets.

Survival

The basic ingredient of glass is silica, derived from sand, flint, or quartz, and combined with other materials in different amounts. In order to facilitate the fusion of the materials an alkali flux is added usually in the form of the carbonates of sodium or potassium. The colour of natural glass is usually green-blue due to the impurities in the raw materials. To obtain a clear, colourless glass manganese is added. When the materials of glass are well balanced the glass is stable, but problems will arise when there is an excess of alkali and low lime. Then the glass will be susceptible to attack by moisture. Old glass with 20-30 per cent sodium or potassium may have 'glass disease', where the glass weeps and begins to break down. In extreme cases where the level of soda is very high the glass could dissolve in water and result in a syrupy fluid.

Sodium and potassium oxides are hygroscopic and will absorb moisture from the air. Depending on the amounts involved, the effect on the glass will differ. In cases where there is a relative humidity (RH) of 40 per cent and above, some items may produce drops of moisture on the surface. In very salty water the sodium and potassium may leach out leaving a fragile and porous surface. The result will be crazing, cracking, flaking or pitting and the surface may have a frosty appearance. In extreme cases the glass may split into layers.

One of the most common effects of corrosion on glass is devitrification. The symptoms are iridescent layers which appear to flake off. It may also have a cloudy, iridescent appearance (see picture) and can appear on glass of all periods, although most glass from the eighteenth century onwards was produced from a stable formula and will not cause many problems.

Glass Flaking

Lead glass recovered from anaerobic conditions may have a very dense black film on the surface. Do not try to remove this but leave for a conservator.

During the period 1880–1914 manganese dioxide was added to glass to keep it clear. When this glass is exposed to ultraviolet light it will slowly turn pink or violet. This is often seen in old telegraph insulators. Glass containing selenium, also used to keep it clear, was used mainly between 1914 and 1930 and often changes to an amber colour.

Care
Examine the glass before washing. If it has been repaired do not get it wet as the adhesive used may disintegrate. Use

only tepid water and never put glass in hot or cold water. The sudden change from room temperature to hot or cold may cause the glass to crack; this is particularly true for old glass. Do not immerse early soda glass in water as it is very soluble and will start to absorb moisture. Potash glass is not so affected by this. Wash gently; do not rub.

Do not leave vessels with stoppers in place to dry as this will cause condensation. Do not store on metal surfaces as the metal can stain or scratch the glass. Glass is affected by light, heat and moisture, so never leave to dry in direct sunlight or near a heat source such as a radiator, cooling vents or strong lighting. Do not subject to sudden changes of temperature, as if taken from a warm environment to a cold one the glass may shatter. Be sure items are completely dry before packing. Label carefully that glass is present, not only so others will take care in handling, but if it is broken in transit there will be a note to take care. Glass should ideally be stored in a RH of 40–50 per cent; avoid damp areas as moisture from the air will cause devitrification.

Glass Survival

Alkaline soils	Neutral soils	Acidic soils
Y	Y	Y
Waterlogged alkaline soils	Waterlogged neutral soils	Waterlogged acidic soils
Y	Y	Y

Organics
Bone

Bone has been used extensively to form artefacts and is comparable in use to our modern plastics. It was a cheap material, easily available and could be carved by anyone with no specialist skills required. Some of the most common artefacts are spoons and pins. The ninth–twelfth centuries were the golden age of bone and antler crafting. Most of the bone utilised was from domesticated animals such as horses, sheep, cattle and pigs, but bird bones were also used for items such as musical pipes. Metapodials, or leg bones which have little meat, are among the most commonly utilised bones. Bone-working areas can be indicated by the presence of the discarded articular ends of long bones.

The makeup of bone is similar to that of ivory and antler and can therefore be easily mistaken for these materials, particularly if the item has been deliberately coloured or has changed colour due to depositional processes. If in doubt use a 10x hand lens to examine the item carefully.

Part of the makeup of bone is a number of cells called osteocytes that are connected to each other, to nerves and blood vessels by thin tubes called canaliculi. When bone grows the osteocytes are swallowed up, forcing them to form new osteocytes and new canaliculi (not always parallel and not continuous). This gives bone its distinct markings, pockmarks (osteocytes) and lines (canaliculi), which often appear on an artefact like 'dots and dashes' (compare this to ivory on page 46). If the piece is broken, look inside the breaks: if it looks a bit like a 'Crunchie' chocolate bar the material is probably bone as these cavities are blood vessels. If the item is not broken put a light behind it (not for long as, if it is ivory, you might damage it) and you may be able to detect the blood vessels.

Uncoloured bone often appears a creamy white and yellows with age. However, when recovered from the ground it can be dark brown, black. It may show discolouration if it has been in contact with metals such as copper or iron, when it will often appear green or reddish respectively. If burnt, bone can be very white or mottled grey with black blemishes. If polished it is more opaque than and not as shiny as ivory.

Survival

Artefacts of bone are very common because it was extensively used and because it survives well in the ground, except in acidic soils.

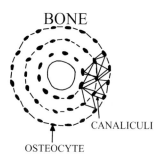

*'Dots' and 'dashes'
of bone*

Care of

Bone that is stable can be cleaned with water and a brush but if it has been recovered in a friable condition and is dry, do not wet. If friable and recovered wet do not allow it to dry out as it will be subject to shrinkage and distortion. If the piece is composite be careful about wetting as associated metals can stain the piece, so take conservation advice.

Bone Survival

Alkaline soils	Neutral soils	Acidic soils
Y	Y	N
Waterlogged alkaline soils	Waterlogged neutral soils	Waterlogged acidic soils
Y	Y	N

Antler

Antler is a fast-growing form of bone which comes from a large variety of deer species. Antlers emerge from a bony lump or protuberance at the top of the skull. In the first year there is only one prong or point but as the animal grows older the antler develops more points, becoming more complex as long as the animal is fit and has access to food.

Antler consists of a beam, or main stem, from which grow a number of branches, tines or points. First to develop is the brow-tine, then the bez-tine followed by the trez-tine after which tines are referred to as just 'points on top'. At the base of the beam the antler is solid and it is from here that small solid items, such as dice, are cut. Further up the beam the core is soft (see picture) and is often cleaned out prior to use. However, when used for handles, such as for a knife, the tang of the blade is hammered into the core where the soft material acts to secure the tang (see page 156). In other artefacts the rough, outer part of the antler is removed leaving the inner surface which may be left white or stained with a colour and/or engraved. The inner surface, when not coloured, looks similar to bone or ivory and is often confused with these materials. Antler is stronger than bone and is often used in artefacts where strength is required. Combs are often made from antler as the teeth can be cut without the fear of breakage; this is unlike bone where the teeth can only be cut with the grain and may break (see page 41).

Antler was either taken from animals that had been killed, or was collected from the wild in early spring after the males had shed their antlers. During medieval times deer, particularly red deer, were the preserve of royal hunting parties, so most of the antler used in artefacts was shed antler. The golden age of antler and bone carving was during the ninth–twelfth centuries. In the archaeological record antler comes from, at most five species of deer: the red, fallow and roe deer as well as elk and reindeer.

Red Deer

Red deer are the most widely distributed deer in the world. The stem of the antlers has a rough, grooved surface with, in Britain, a maximum of 12-14 smooth tines and there is no palmation as seen on the fallow deer, reindeer or elk. The red deer was the ultimate hunt animal and it is usually the one portrayed in early art. The antler was used almost completely with little discarded and is often found in early medieval urban manufacturing centres. The antler head-dress from the early Mesolithic site at Star Carr is of red deer.

Fallow Deer

Male fallow antlers are smoother than the red or the roe deer and tend not to have a bez-tine. They have palmate (flattened) areas on the upper parts above the trez-tine. The fallow is not native to Britain but was introduced around the eleventh century, probably by the Normans.

Roe Deer

Roe are very small deer, about the size of a large goat, and the males have the simplest antlers consisting of a relatively straight slender beam rising almost vertically from the head, covered with tiny bony nodules. There are two or more points on top. Roe deer have been in Britain since the last glaciation but suffered a decline in the medieval period. Turner, quoted in MacGregor (see page 32), states that in some areas this may be due to a law of 1339-40, which rduced the roe deer from a beast of the forest, which meant it could only be hunted by royals, to a beast of the warren, which meant it could be hunted by anyone. However, there were other considerations, such as its disappearing habitat when forests were being cut down to create farmland.

Reindeer

Reindeer antlers are found on both sexes, unlike the roe, fallow and red deer, where they are only found on the males. The beam sweeps backwards and upwards and the upper points are palmate. The surface is very smooth with only slight grooves: two sets, one in the front and one at the back, are common. Reindeer antler was one of the most important raw materials for Palaeolithic people.

Elk

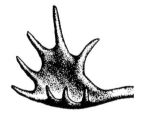

Elk probably disappeared from Britain during the Mesolithic. Its antlers are enormous palmates at right angles to the animal's face with the points surrounding the palmate facing upwards. A number of perforated mattock heads possibly for digging have been found. Two elk skulls and antlers were found at Star Carr.

Survival

Artefacts of antler, like bone, are very common because antler was so extensively used but also because it survives well in the ground, except in acidic soils.

Care

Antler can be cleaned with water and a brush but if it has been recovered in a friable condition and is dry, do not wet. If friable and recovered wet do not allow it to dry out as it will be subject to shrinkage and distortion. If the piece is composite be careful about wetting, as associated metals can stain the piece. Take conservation advice.

Antler Survival

Alkaline soils	Neutral soils	Acidic soils
Y	Y	N
Waterlogged alkaline soils	Waterlogged neutral soils	Waterlogged acidic soils
N	Y	Y

Horn

Horn rarely survives in the ground and so is not covered in detail here.

Horn Survival

Alkaline soils	Neutral soils	Acidic soils
N	N	N
Waterlogged alkaline soils	Waterlogged neutral soils	Waterlogged acidic soils
N	Y	Y

Ivory

Ivory is basically dentine, the same substance from which teeth are made. Artefacts have been made from ivory since prehistoric times when mammoth tusks were used. Since then artefacts have been made from five natural ivories and two synthetic ivories, as listed below.

Dentine is very similar to bone (see above), but the osteocyte cells are called odontoblasts. The odontoblasts remain on the inside edge, near the pulp cavity, and deposit dentine in tubules which stretch in long lines to the outside

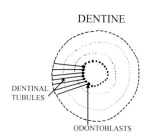

DENTINE

DENTINAL TUBULES

ODONTOBLASTS

edge of the tusk. This gives ivory its distinct markings, namely its long lines, the length of which are usually consistent but do depend on the radius of the tusk. The lines form different patterns in different ivories.

Ivory is denser than bone and will be heavier than a comparably sized bone piece; it is also slightly softer. It will not burn white like bone but chars black, and as bone ages it yellows, whereas ivory tends to get whiter. A large bone item may display the typical curve of bone at the back, while ivory tends to be flat on the back, particularly in jewellery.

Elephant and mammoth ivory

The purest primary dentine, and the only ivory regarded as 'true', is that of the elephant and mammoth, although a number of other substances have been called 'ivory'. There are a lot of mammoth ivory artefacts around, as from the seventeenth century onwards there has been a huge trade from the vast 'mammoth cemeteries' in Alaska and Siberia that usually come to light in the spring melt. As a very rough guide to tell elephant from mammoth: look closely at the lines. As no tusk is ever a true circle the lines will be elliptical and cross over forming an intersection called cross-hatching. In mammoth ivory they form an acute angle, averaging 90° or less. In the elephant the angle is 115° or higher.

Mammoth ivory

Elephant ivory

Walrus ivory

After elephant ivory, walrus is the most important in an archaeological context as it has regularly been used from late Saxon times when it was referred to as morse ivory.

From the late tenth to the thirteenth centuries walrus ivory was used extensively for secular and devotional objects, as it was plentiful due to expanding trade with Scandinavia during a corresponding difficulty in procuring elephant ivory at this time. Probably the most famous walrus ivory is the Lewis chess set in the British Museum.

Walrus ivory is less dense than elephant ivory and more oval in cross section. It appears in layers, the first being a thick cementum covering that needs to be removed before

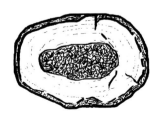

the ivory can be accessed. A small transition ring separates the cementum from the dentine and there are fine longitudinal cracks that start at the cementum and penetrate inwards through the dentine and appear down the length of the tusk. The ivory is then split into two primary dentine layers. The first is pretty featureless but when fresh is similar in colour, translucency and hardness to elephant ivory. The secondary dentine is the dark inner core that is unique to the walrus. It has a high mineral content with whorls, and artefacts made from this layer tend to take on a marbled look. This hard osteo-dentine was sometimes used for weapon hilts and drinking cups, as it was believed walrus ivory could cure the effects of poison and any wounds received in battle. At York's main archaeological sites, many of the ivories discovered were made of secondary dentine.

Hippopotamus Ivory

Hippopotamus ivory's fine grain makes it harder to carve than elephant ivory; in fact it is the hardest of the ivories. However, it is less prone to decay, which often made it more expensive. Its durability had recommended it from Phoenician times onwards for false teeth. The earliest example of this use dates from between the sixth–fourth century BC: two carved ivory teeth held together by gold wire. The most famous example is the set worn by George Washington. Due to the limited size of the tusks, hippo ivory was used predominantly to make small flat items, such as buttons and inlays, although it is often seen in umbrella, stick and door handles and pyx boxes.

Other ivories

Narwhal ivory (the origin of the unicorn legend) was used extensively throughout the fifteenth and sixteenth centuries but as much of it was ground down for powder little has been left from antiquity. The Japanese used it extensively for *netsuke* (small figurines).

From *c*.1865 vegetable ivory became very popular. It comes from the inner nut of about 20 palm species distributed along tropical rivers. The nuts have a series of regularly spaced concentric lines which on larger specimens can be seen with the naked eye, or otherwise under a magnifying glass. The lines travel in one direction and follow the curve of the nut and serve a similar purpose to the dentinal lines of true ivory, to supply oil. The lines are often difficult to identify in an object for, being so fine, they are practically indistinguishable in a polished piece. It is mainly used for small items: jewellery, thimbles, thimble cases, tape measures, dice, rings, ornaments, chess pieces, reeds for wind instruments, piano keys, billiard balls, umbrella handles, and small ornaments including *netsuke*. Much expensive Victorian 'ivory' jewellery was in fact vegetable ivory passed off as elephant ivory. The greatest utilisation and consumption of vegetable ivory was in the production of buttons. By 1887 factories in London and Birmingham alone were using some 2–3 million nuts a year. Since then plastics or synthetic ivories have largely replaced vegetable ivory.

Due to the dwindling supply of elephant ivory a reward was offered for anyone to come up with a synthetic ivory. In 1865 Alexander Parkes invented a synthetic ivory using celluloid that has since been called French Ivory, Ivoride, Genuine French Ivory, Ivorine and a host of other names. Synthetic ivories usually do not have the same sheen and 'naturalness' of real ivory. Early fake grain patterns were pressed onto the surface to imitate the lines in elephant ivory. Later, cross-hatching was added as well so that it is extremely difficult to tell fake ivory from real. A general rule is that the effects tend to be smoother and regular in the fake and more irregular in real ivory. In instances of very good imitations, chemical tests are required to tell real ivory and fakes apart. In synthetic ivory, look for traces of mould marks and air bubbles and a texture that feels 'rougher' than true ivory. Genuine ivory may feel colder than a synthetic material as ivory conducts heat more efficiently.

Survival

Ivory survives reasonably well.

Care

Ivory is notoriously sensitive to heat, light and moisture so when cleaning, bear the following in mind: use clean, cool or lukewarm (not hot) water. Do not immerse, or soak the piece in water but try to keep as dry as possible. Do not use a toothbrush or anything that may mark the piece, instead use the fingers or a soft cloth but not one that can snag easily.

Ivory will warp and split if subjected to any sudden change of environment. If it has been removed from a wet context then it should be kept wet and cool until it can be conserved properly. It is important that, if there is any doubt about the identification of wet ivory, it should be immediately suspended in clean water until a specialist can examine it (if it turns out to be bone the water will have caused the bone no harm). The water should just cover the item (not 'drown' it) and it should be checked regularly to ensure that excessive evaporation has not taken place.

If the piece comes from a dry environment do not put it in water but leave to air dry in a steady environment without too much fluctuation of temperature. Do not leave near a heat source as this can lead to warping and cracking, nor place it next to a window in case of direct sunlight.

Ivory Survival

Alkaline soils	Neutral soils	Acidic soils
Y	Y	N
Waterlogged alkaline soils	Waterlogged neutral soils	Waterlogged acidic soils
Y	Y	N

Wood

Wood has been used extensively throughout history not only for manufacturing items but also for fuel, drugs and food. Wood management has occurred since the Neolithic times to ensure a continuous supply and therefore the recovery of wooden items in favourable conditions is fairly common. However, the recovery record is skewed by the fact that many pieces would not have been discarded but used as fuel. Evidence of wood may exist, not only as items in themselves but also as impressions in clay based items such as daub for buildings and building material which has been laid on wood to dry. If the impression is clear enough it may be possible to identify the species.

Before the 1800s, wood was hand-sawn and on unfinished wood, particularly on the backs of larger pieces, straight marks may be seen to indicate hand sawing. The circular saw was not introduced until the end of the eighteenth century and can be identified on unfinished wood with circular marks.

Survival

Due to the damp conditions of British soils wood artefacts are often difficult to recover intact. However, they may be found in dry conditions such as standing buildings or caves where they have been shielded from the elements. Often wood is recovered from anaerobic waterlogged conditions, which may be present on any site in the form of wells, ponds or ditches. In waterlogged environments oxygen is precluded which means that the organisms which feed on organic materials cannot survive.

If the piece recovered is large enough it may be possible to identify the species, and if particularly large dendrochronology (the dating of wood using tree rings) may be possible.

Care

Always be aware of the possibility of wood in composite items. Before cleaning a check should be made that there is no wooden residue in hafts, sockets and other openings where a wooden handle or the like may have existed.

Do not get dry wood wet. If encrusted with earth, brush lightly with a soft brush, but do not use any force, as if the wood is soft, brush marks may be left, possibly obscuring information. Alternatively wipe with a damp cloth, being careful not to immerse the piece in water.

If recovered wet do not allow the object to dry out as it will warp, splinter and crack. Wet wood must be kept wet. Place in a secure polythene bag and cover with clean, cool water and store in a cool, dark environment. Make sure the water does not evaporate, nor mould grow, by monitoring daily.

If the artefact is too large, or is in a position where it cannot be immediately removed from the site, it should be sprayed regularly and covered with a plastic sheet. Try to keep it out of direct sunlight. Waterlogged wood will retain its shape as long as it remains wet, but when lifting, keep the piece supported evenly at all times as it will easily fall apart if lifted by its side or end.

As soon as possible remove all wooden items for conservation as they will need to be treated with a liquid wax, polyethylene glycol (PEG), which will replace the cells in the wood and help maintain the shape of the object. The piece will then be freeze-dried, making it stable enough for display.

Wood Survival

Alkaline soils	Neutral soils	Acidic soils
Y	Y	N
Waterlogged alkaline soils	Waterlogged neutral soils	Waterlogged acidic soils
Y	Y	N

Jet

Jet is fossilised wood. It is black, opaque, and has a resinous lustre that can be highly polished. Being a poor conductor it is warm to the touch and when rubbed vigorously static electricity will be generated causing dust mites and fibres to adhere to it, which must have seemed quite magical in antiquity. When rubbed on a piece of unglazed porcelain it leaves a brown streak. It has a high carbon content and so, like coal, will easily burn. Despite a similar appearance to coal it is extremely light in weight. It breaks easily and when it does so it fractures in a conchoidal manner (for more on conchoidal fracture see page 60).

The earliest known use of jet in Britain was in the Neolithic period but it was not used much until the Bronze Age, as it is a quite hard material and needs strong tools to carve it. By the Bronze Age there are items such as beads, V-shaped perforated buttons and conical studs. Perhaps the best-known Bronze Age find is a necklace of over one hundred beads found in 1928 at Kill y Kiaran, Scotland and on display at the Nation Museums of Scotland, Edinburgh. Roman jet artefacts exist from the second century AD but on the whole tend to date to the third and fourth centuries, declining towards the end of the occupation. Jet was believed to have medicinal properties, particularly anaesthetising powers and as an antidote to poison, which may explain its popularity in cutlery handles. During the Viking and Saxon periods jet was not as common as it was in Roman times. However, during the ninth century, jet was exported from Jorvik (York) and has been found in Norway, Sweden, Finland and Denmark. Throughout the medieval period jet was often utilised by the Church for items such as rosaries and crucifixes, as it was believed to ward off the 'evil eye'.

Much British jet came from the North York Moors and in particular from Whitby. However, by the end of the nineteenth century, Whitby jet was exhausted and was superseded by imports from France and Spain.

Survival

Jet survives in most soil conditions but particularly well in waterlogged conditions. Upon recoverey it looks black and shiny.

Cleaning

Do not get dry jet wet, but wipe with a damp cloth if necessary. Do not immerse it in water. Allow to air dry and do not subject it to any heat source, e.g. drying near a radiator. Allow it to dry away from sharp objects as it is easily scratched. Store separately for the same reason, and when packing use polythene foam as a backing.

Jet Survival

Alkaline soils	Neutral soils	Acidic soils
Y	Y	Y
Waterlogged alkaline soils	Waterlogged neutral soils	Waterlogged acidic soils
Y	Y	Y

Leather

Leather has been an essential part of culture throughout history and has been used for numerous purposes, even including coins. The Chinese had a leather coinage in the second century BC, as did the Romans. In fact the word *pecuniary* (monetary) comes from the Latin *pecus*, meaning 'hide' (as late as the First World War, leather coins were used in Germany). The Romans used leather on a wide scale and it is frequently recovered in excavations. Leather usage increased over time and by medieval times most towns would have had their own tannery, usually situated out of town due to the stench of the tanning process, and near a water source. A legacy of the presence of tanneriesmay still be seen in street names such as Tanner Street, Bark Street and Leather Lane. The most desired leather in medieval times was a goatskin made by the Arabs and known as morocco leather. The name is still a measure of quality leather.

Composition

Skins are divided into two categories: hides which come from larger animals such as cattle and horse, and skins which come from smaller ones such as sheep, goats and pigs. Animal skin consists of three layers:

1. The epidermis or outer layer which consists of a thin layer of cells and the hair. This layer is removed before

tanning, often by scraping using an implement such as a flint scraper (see page 67).

2. The corium or middle layer (also called the grain layer) consisting of a dense layer of collagen protein fibres which gives skin its strength, elasticity and durability. As the animal ages the corium increases in thickness and density. This is why the skin from young animals, such as calfskin, which is thinner and softer, was used for parchment and vellum. In addition the thickness and density of the corium varies between the sexes, with those of the bulls being thick, tough, coarse-grained and very strong. These thick hides are usually split lengthwise, the upper layers being used as grain leather whilst the lower, or flesh side, are used for suede leather.

3. The flesh or bottom layer from which fat or meat was also scraped off.

Tanning

Skins contain approximately 60–65 per cent water, 25–30 per cent protein and 5–10 per cent fats. When an animal dies the skin beings to lose water and becomes inflexible and stiff. To prevent this natural decay it needs to be tanned, to convert it into leather.

It is not known when tanning began, but Utzi, the Iceman (from c.5000 BC), found in the Italian Alps, had tanned leather.

Survival

Leather will survive well in low oxygen conditions such as waterlogged or very dry environments.

Care

Leather is a difficult material to conserve particularly when it is part of a composite artefact with metal. Fats in the leather will accelerate the corrosion of metals and may be seen as a turquoise, waxy substance on copper. If this is present then conservation advice is needed.

If recovered dry do not wet leather as it can harden as it dries out, leaving discoloured areas where the piece was made wet. If available, use a low-powered hand vacuum cleaner with a gauze or a fine netting over the nozzle so no parts are accidentally lost. If not, then brush with a soft brush. Do not use a hard brush as this may leave marks.

Wet leather should be cleaned with either the fingers whilst wearing disposable latex gloves, a soft water jet, or a sponge but nothing that may mark the item.

If there are stains do not attempt to remove them. Also with complex artefacts it may be advisable to remove only the surface dirt and not to attempt to clean in areas where the structure of the item may be compromised, for example shoes which are multi-layer (see page 174).

Do not use commercial oils or soaps on dry leather as once applied they cannot be easily removed and will contravene conservation advice that nothing may be used on an item that cannot be reversed, and whose removal may damage the object. They may also cause changes in colour due to different wearing and aging and if overused oils can encourage mould as it provides nutrients.

Do not leave to dry near a heat source as this will dry the leather out too quickly, causing it to crack and become brittle. Do not leave to dry near a light source as fading is a high possibility.

Do not fold leather, or rest it on an edge (for example propping it up to dry). Leather must be fully supported so it does not distort.

Packing

Do not store dry leather in sealed bags becuase of the risk of condensation. Make sure the bag is well ventilated by piercing with holes. A stationery hole punch is ideal for this purpose. Then place inside a black bin liner so it is away from the light. When storing wet leather place in a stong polythene bag. Cover the items with water but do not 'drown' them, and store in black bin bags. If possible, keep the bags in containers such as buckets to provide a support for the items. Do not over-pack individual bags as they will burst, as well as being too heavy too move. Monitor the water level in the bags regularly for evaporation and mould. If necessary change the water regularly. Do not add fungicides or any other chemicals despite advice in various books as fungicide may interfere with carbon-14 dating if required. It may also form uneven deposits on the leather after freeze-drying. Furthermore, amounts are difficult to estimate and if too much is used this may cause hazards not only to those processing the leather but also to those who work on the leather at a later date, such as the conservators.

Storing

Dust is particularly damaging to leather as the particles can scratch the surface. Also dust acts as a magnet for moisture and will accelerate fungal growth. Store items in black bin liners or with a covering to protect from dust settling on them.

Leather is very susceptible to changes in humidity and high humidity will encourage the growth of mould that may stain the leather or cause distortions. If long-term storage for dried leather is unavoidable then it should be stored in a relative humidity (RH) within the range of 45–55 per cent. If the RH is below 30 per cent, leather will dry out, while above 65 per cent mould will grow. The temperature should ideally be kept to 18–22°C.

Leather Survival

Alkaline soils	Neutral soils	Acidic soils
N	N	N
Waterlogged alkaline soils	Waterlogged neutral soils	Waterlogged acidic soils
Y	Y	Y

Chapter 2

FLINT

Identifying worked flint

Flint is a common stone in south-east England. In some places it is found in proximity to chalk, embedded within the chalk as nodules or in layers of tabular flint. In other places it occurs as pebbles or nodules scattered in topsoils from which chalk has been eroded or as stray pieces transported by glaciers during the last Ice Age. These stray nodules were often the basis for early tools. During the Neolithic period, flint mines such as Cissbury and Findon in Sussex and Grimes Graves on the Suffolk/Norfolk border were worked to provide first-class flint. Neolithic axes that were used to fell trees needed the strength that pristine flint has. Most prehistoric lithics are made from flint, although chert (another name for flint but recovered from non-chalk areas) has been used, as well as other rocks.

The reason flint was used extensively is that it is a material that will fracture according to design. It is reasonably strong and can produce sharp cutting edges and points. The colour of flint is often black with many variations such as dark brown, yellow, red or white but some may have different colours within one piece. Flint contains a fair proportion of moisture and when in the ground for prolonged periods of time, can absorb surrounding minerals and

Proximal End

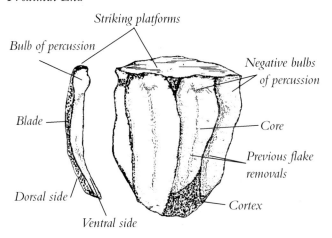

Distal End

chemicals, thereby changing colour. This colouring is the patina. The outer surface of flint often has a cortex, or skin, that varies in thickness and colour. From flint blocks recovered in, or near, chalk have a cortex that often exhibits the bright whiteness of chalk.

When flint is burnt it takes on a different characteristic. It may appear very white, grey or black with crazed lines all over the surface.

Chert is similar to the flaking properties of flint but control of flaking is not so fine and finished shapes tend to be rougher in shape and finish.

When a blow is directed vertically at the edge of a block of flint the energy from the blow will travel in all directions through the block until it meets the edges of the block and fractures. The piece of flint on the external side of the fracture will fall away producing a flake. As the resulting flake resembles a limpet shell it is called a *conchoidal* fracture (*conchoid* from the Latin for impet).

Proximal End

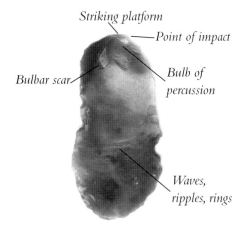

Striking platform

Point of impact

Bulbar scar

Bulb of percussion

Waves, ripples, rings

Distal End

©PAS

Identifying a struck flake

The front, or ventral, side of the flake (the surface that was attached to the core) will exhibit a record of the blow made on the core. The face of the flake will be fairly flat and smooth with the following characteristics:

The point of impact: a slight crushing where the blow landed.

Fissure marks: there may be a number of straight fissures which look like scratch marks emanating from the bulbar scar.

The bulb of percussion: (This can also be found on natural flints when they are struck by other rocks. Therefore the identification of struck flints should be made on as many characteristics as possible, rather than relying on one feature.) Prominent bulbs of percussion are often the result of using a hard hammer (such as a stone) and diffuse bulbs the result of a soft hammer (such as antler or bone). However, these cannot always be taken as firm evidence as both are possible from each method.

The bulb is the prime indicator that identifies the ventral side of the flake, as well as the proximal end.

Waves, ripples or rings: These radiate from the point of impact as shock waves from the blow. As these waves are concave relative to the bulb of percussion, if the bulb is absent it is possible to tell from the waves which is the proximal end. On the ventral surface of the flake they will appear in positive relief, on the core they appear in negative relief.

Flint choppers and axes

Stone tools can be up to 2.6 million years old. They are the first known tools to be modified by humans rather than simply utilised in their natural form, and originally consisted of pebbles crudely adapted to provide a cutting edge. These pebble tools originated in Africa (the most famous being the Oldowan, named after after Olduvia Gorge where they were first recognised) and spread around the world from the Lower Palaeolithic and later. They are not in evidence much after the Middle Palaeolithic. One of the difficulties in recovery is that they are often confused with debitage (waste flint work). For about 500,000 years choppers were the dominant tool until the design was modified into the more efficient handaxe.

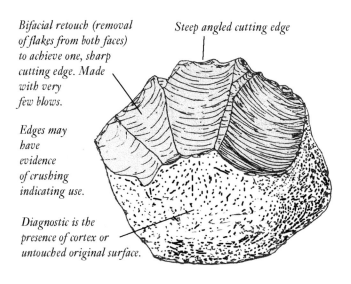

Bifacial retouch (removal of flakes from both faces) to achieve one, sharp cutting edge. Made with very few blows.

Edges may have evidence of crushing indicating use.

Diagnostic is the presence of cortex or untouched original surface.

Steep angled cutting edge

Pebble tools are thick and heavy with minimal working. There are numerous varieties and sizes, although most were of a size to fit neatly into the hand (most average between 50mm and 120mm), and are for the most part dependent on the form of the original pebble

Narrows towards the top (distal end)

Good cutting edges all around the tool

Pointed handaxes were not much use for digging – a stick was better

For the first time shallow flaking appears and covers much of the two faces

Edges generally straight

Heavy butt that fits into the hand. Handaxes may not always be completely worked, some cortex may remain and occasionally they are mistaken for choppers

Other shapes of handaxe may have rounded, not pointed, tops

Size varies but most are about 10 cm long. However large examples have been found such as the 15.24cm long x 6.35cm wide Acheulean handaxe from Norfolk. Some are too heavy, and too well made to be of practical use and may therefore have been symbolic

Handaxes

The technological innovations of the Lower Palaeolithic enabled the production of tools to a pre-determined shape by removing smaller flakes than those needed to make a chopper. More control was then gained over the finished item. The newly developed handaxe was a prime example and there are many standardised forms, although the pointed, ovate and cordate were the most popular. Another innovation was secondary flaking. The handaxe was roughed out (usually with a hard hammer) and then retouched, often over the whole surface, with a soft hammer. The classification of handaxes (also called bifaces) is based on their shape, which included almond, ovate and pear to name a few (the term 'axe' does not denote the same tool as we are familiar with and the true axe did not appear until Mesolithic). Handaxe production lasted for over a million years and is spread over much of the world, although most axes have local diagnostic features. By the Mesolithic the handaxe was being replaced with a wider selection of tools produced in response to new hunting practices.

Ovate Handaxe
A continuous cutting edge but more oval. From the Lower Palaeolithic and probably the most favoured handaxe

Cordate handaxe
A thin cutting edge all around. From the Lower Palaeolithic

Mesolithic axes and adzes

At the end of the Palaeolithic, handaxes disappeared and were replaced by the axe typical of the Mesolithic: the heavy, trenchet axe, and the first true axe. It was shaped and sharpened by removing a long flake across the cutting edge with a transverse blow to the axe. It was probably hafted with antler or wood. Various books refer to the 'Thames Pick' – this term is no longer used as it is generally seen as a trenchet axe.

Trenchet Axe

Ranges from 2cm to over 40cm, the larger varieties were probably to deal with forest clearances.

One or both sides will be concave in profile giving it a triangular shape in profile. Edge is uneven and thin due to flakes being taken off from both sides.

Flake removed is either to shape the tool, or to sharpen it. Axe sharpening flakes vary but above is a diagnostic flake for Mesolithic trenchet axes.

Non-Trenchet Axe

Axes very similar to the trenchet were also used during the Mesolithic. The basic difference is that rather than having a trenchet flake being removed, the edges are retouched. This results in a more ovate profile.

Pick

Picks can sometimes be mistaken for axes as they share a similar form. However, rather than cutting they were probably more used for digging in the ground, for this purpose the pick will have a pointed end. Usually the width of the point will be approximately 3 cms. The point can be triangular, diamond-shaped or sub-circular.

Most are less than 12cm, the profile is more triangular or quadrilateral.

Hafting

Hafting would have been done in a wooden (often ash or oak as these absorb impact better) or antler handle secured with leather thongs to tighten

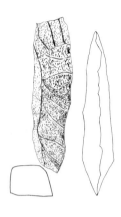

Adze

An adze is similar to the axes but the under surface is flat and the working edge is angled downwards. They were probably hafted with working edge at right angles to handle and used for dressing wood. The edge of abn adze is a shape whereas an axe has a shape.

The blade of an axe is parallel to the handle along its axis. An adze blade however is perpendicular to the vertical of the handle and turned towards it. Cousin of the hoe, it was used to hollow out canoes, flatten wood to make the smooth surface of a plank

Profile

The profile of the Mesolithic celt and adze tends to be slightly sinuous or zigzag due to the manufacturing technique of alternative flaking (flakes are removed alternatively from each side). Compare this to the straighter edge of the Neolithic celt (page 44).

Neolithic axes

During the Neolithic a number of different types of axe were used and shaped according to their usage, such as adze, chisel and gouge. The most diagnostic of the Neolithic is the polished axe, the earliest of which has been found at the Somerset Trackway dating from the Early Neolithic, c.4000 BC. These required a great deal of time to create as they needed to be rubbed against a stationary rubber block of abrasive stone such as quartz sandstone, using water as a lubricant. A number of these blocks with depressions have been found. This new technique of manufacture coincided with the advent of agriculture and the new tool was probably most used to fell small trees (larger ones were probably culled with fire). The smooth cutting edge gave the axe greater strength; flaked tools are weaker because of the uneven distribution of stress. Also, the head penetrates deeper than a flaked axe. Some are of great beauty; others are so thin as to be of no practical use, so must have had a more symbolic purpose.

They were traded over great distances throughout Europe and are made from a range of stones, including greenstone (from Mount's Bay in Cornwall), volcanic ash, grey stone (from Graig Lwyd, Wales), jadeite and other hard rocks.

Not all Neolithic axes were polished. Flaked axes continued in production although some may have had the cutting edge alone polished. Polished stone axes vary in size and shape from around 2cm to over 40cm.

The Neolithic celt profile is straighter than that of the Mesolithic (see page 64). This is becuase flakes were removed from down one side and then the other rather than from alternate sides as in the Mesolithic.
Polished axes are often faceted on the side

Generally a flake is more than twice as long as it is wide and they appear sporadically before the Upper Palaeolithic

Flint flakes and flake tools

Flakes are pieces of flint that have been removed, intentionally or otherwise, from a core. During the roughing- out stage when making cores, axes, etc. the flakes removed are 'primary' flakes and are usually characterised by a pronounced bulb of percussion from the use of a hard hammer. Once the piece has been roughed out and further work is needed, the flakes removed at this stage are 'secondary' and are often characterised by a defused bulb of percussion as they are usually struck with a soft hammer and tend to be thinner than primary flakes. However, in both cases either a soft or hard hammer may be used. Most flakes have razor sharp edges and are ready to be used as cutting implements without any further work. They fall into three categories:

a) waste or debitage: those pieces that have been removed during the shaping or sharpening, and not utilised

b) utilised flakes, those that have been used but not modified

Usually made on the side of a flake, a denticulate is a series of small notches along the edge. The tool is used as a kind of saw

One of the earliest diagnostic flakes is the Clactonian. These were both utilised and reworked, particularly into scraping, chopping and cutting tools.

Clactonian flakes are often thick, heavy, squat and vary in size up to around 15cm. They are invariable struck with a hard hammer and have a characteristic large bulb of percussion and a thick butt

c) blanks, those which were intended to be modified into a tool

d) retouched flakes, those that have received secondary working to turn them into tools.

The Levallois flake

The advantage of the Levallois technique (see page 69) is that flakes are made to a predetermined shape (size and shape vary according to core preparation) and require little further work, although there may be some retouching on the butt for holding or hafting. The Levallois technique provides a more economical use of resources.

The core yields only one long flake (right), which can have the appearance of an ovate handaxe, and will be flat, thin and disc-shaped, bearing the scars of the previous flaking from stage two whilst the underside will be smooth.

The bulb of percussion will be at the edge where it was detached from the platform in stage four.

Flake scrapers: (see also blade scrapers page 74)

©PAS   ©PAS

Side scrapers

A scraper with retouch on the edge of a blade or flake. There are numerous types of side scraper but generally they are retouched on one or both edges. As with end scrapers, side scrapers can be either convex or concave. The benefit of a side scraper is that there is a longer, straighter edge

Transverse scraper
A convex end scraper made on a flake that is wider than it is long

Round scrapers

As the name suggests, these are round pieces of flint with part, or all, of the edge retouched, and of various sizes and shapes.

Very common on Mesolithic sites are small round thumb-nail scrapers which are usually less than 2cm in diameter.

©PAS

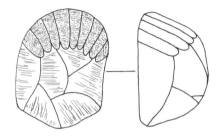

Carinate scraper

Made on heavy flakes with thick, steep edges.

Nose scraper

Like the carinated scraper, the nose scraper is made on heavy flakes with thick steep edges, with a protrusion pinched in on both sides so that it resembles a nose. They are common in the Upper Palaeolithic but rarer in the Mesolithic.

Flint cores

A core is the original block of flint from which flakes, blades and bladelets are removed. The core itself can be used as an artefact and these become 'core tools'. Cores are rejuvenated by detaching a secondary block from the striking platform. Once the core has been exhausted, and is not reused, it becomes debitage. Core technology provided a large quantity of sharp, straight cutting edges from small amounts of flint so increased efficiency enormously. The detached blades could be used by themselves or as composite tools, and blades could be worked into new tools.

Any piece of flint that has removals can be deemed a core and there are a number of types, usually classified according to the number of striking platforms it has. However, only the basic types are included here.

The Levallois technique

The earliest of the core technologies is the Levallois which appeared in the Upper Palaeolithic and spread worldwide. The core was prepared in four stages:

Stage one A cobble is trimmed into a rough shape by removing flakes from the edges.

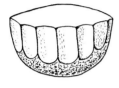

Stage two The upper surface of the core is trimmed from the edge towards the centre, to produce a ridge running along the upper length of the core.

Stage three A platform is prepared from one end of the core to produce an even, flat striking platform for the blow that will detach the flake.

Stage four Finally, the end of the core is struck on the platform, driving a longitudinal flake off the core following the longitudinal ridge (for more on the flake see page 66). The core would then be discarded.

The core is left with a depression where the flake was. The shape of the resulting core has attracted the name 'tortoise-core'.

The most common type of core found is the blade core, which appears in the Upper Palaeolithic. They are distinguished by one or more flat striking platforms and convex depressions where the blades once sat. As they are detached the concave shape leaves ridges on each side which stand proud from the core. The knapper then chooses to either knap directly on to the ridge or between the ridges. If the blow is directed above a ridge this produces a single-ridged blade.

As the blades are detached the core becomes fluted, resulting in a conical or prismatic form, and the more that are detached the more difficult it becomes to detach further blades. Therefore the core needs to be rejuvenated. To facilitate this, a blow is struck at the top of the length of the core and a flake is detached to provide an obtuse angle. The resulting flakes are wedge-shaped and are debitage, or waste.

Conical (prismatic) blade core

Fluted profile

Flat striking platform

Ridge appears centrally on the back of the blade. Can be single-ridged or double-ridged (see also gunflints, page 78)

Long, narrow blades are removed from around the circumference of the core

As more blades are removed the core tapers, making it difficult to detach blades. It therefore needs to be rejuvenated. A blow is aimed at the top to detach a flake and so provide more of an obtuse angle. These wedge-shaped flakes are debitage, or waste

Some may taper to a point; othersmay be more cylindrical

Conical microblade core

Like the conical (prismatic) core, the conical microblade core is for the production of very small blades so is small often no more than 2.54cm high.

This type is found only in the Mesolithic, particularly the early period for during the later Mesolithic longer blades were used to make microliths (see page 77).

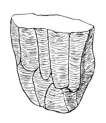

Cylindrical blade core
First platform for the removal of blades

Blades areremoved from around the core

Second, opposing platform often only to straighten up core and correct errors

Flint blades and blade tools

Flakes that are more than twice as long as they are wide, with edges that are approximately parallel, are usually defined as blades. They appeared sporadically before the Upper Palaeolithic but with the introduction of prepared cores became common as they were an efficient way of producing the maximum amount of cutting edge from a flint block. Blade tools are often multifunctional with, for example, a scraper at one end and a burin on the other.

The ridge provides the strength in giving the blade a triangular or trapezoidal cross-section

Due to the strength provided by the ridge, blades could be long, thin and narrow and yet withstand much usage. Blade technology increased the efficiency of raw material usage by some 100 per cent and the narrower a blade was the more, could be struck from one core

A blade tends to be symmetrical and has relatively even, parallel sides

The hallmark of the Upper Palaeolithic blades is their long, narrow and rectangular to triangular shape

Later blades tend to be broader and shorter than those of the Upper Palaeolithic

Small blades, or bladelets tend to be 5mm-12.7mm long

The shape of a blade depends on the way it has been struck from the core. A blow directly above the ridge on the core will result in a single ridged blade (above) (see Cores, page 68). Double ridged or crested blades can be specially prepared (see Gunflints, page 78) which give the blade more strength. A multi-faceted blade can result from a worked core, particularly when it has been worked from both ends

Backed blades

Backed blades are those which have received retouch to blunt one edge, usually to protect the finger during use. Flint knives are often made this way.

Backed blades take many forms but two distinctive types from the Upper Palaeolithic are the Cheddar and Creswell blades which have an angular shape.

The Creswell point is sub-triangular, obliquely blunted with backing down one side and sometimes round the blade end. The Creswell has a single angle on the blunted edge.

The Cheddarian point is basically trapezoidal in shape with retouch on the two oblique ends and backing all or part of the way down one side producing a trapezoidal shape.

Increased use of materials such ivory, antler and bone resulted in a change in and specialisation of blade tools, which were to become numerous. Techniques such as groove and splintering, to produce slivers of bone which could be made into needles, harpoons etc. saw an increase in the types of tool with sharp points such as burins and awls to pierce holes in clothing and other materials.

Bear in mind that by the time a burin, or any other lithic tool, has been used, it may look completely different from when it was first made.

Piercers and borers are tools that have been retouched to a sharp point for making holes in soft materials such as leather. They can be made on a flake, a blade or a core.

Break burin
*A single crested blade
has been snapped.
A blow has been struck
downwards on the right
side edge of blade to
remove a tiny piece of
flint. The waste piece is
the burin spall*

Diherdral burin
*Two opposing removals
resulting in straight,
pointed edge*

©PAS

Burins

Most commonly compared to a chisel, burins were used from the Upper Palaeolithic onwards for scoring grooves, in processes like the groove and splinter technique where lines are cut into a hard material (e.g. bone) and a splinter is levered out to be reworked into a tool such as a needle or pin. Burins could also be used to engrave lines for pictures or patterns on bone, antler, ivory etc. During the Upper Palaeolithic the burin became an effective tool and became extremely numerous in later periods. There is a wide variety of burins; however, all have one or more small, sharp, chisel-like edges.

Awls

Awls first appear in the Upper Palaeolithic and are similar to drills, piercers and borers. They are made with a spike-like point for boring holes in hard materials such as bone, wood or ivory. The spike can be on the end of a blade of flake or on the side and is made by retouching one notch or two to provide the point.

In order to make a hole the tool is used either in a circular movement or back and forward movement, or a combination of both.

The point of an awl tends to be longer than that of a burin and the spike may be smooth from the abrasion of turning.

Scrapers

Scrapers were extremely common from the Middle Palaeolithic onwards and were used to scrape hides, hollow out wood or bone, remove bark from wood, etc. They are usually made on flakes (but also on blades) with no other modification than a row of flake scars to create a thick, wide-angled edge to enable a scraping action. The thickened edge provided greater strength and did not tear the material. Most would have been mounted in a handle but are rarely found this way. With use the scraper becomes progressively blunter and so is resharpened, making the scraper smaller and smaller until it becomes useless and is discarded. Consequently scrapers are found in many sizes.

There are two main types of scrapers: the end scraper and the side scraper. Within these categories there are many other sub-classifications.

See also flake scrapers (page 67).

End scrapers

Scrapers that are made on either, or both, the proximal or distal end of a flake or blade. Most, however, are made on the distal end, to avoid the removal of the bulb of percussion. End scrapers are then categorised according to the shape of the retouched edge as straight, concave or convex.

Convex End Scrapers

The dorsal side bears the scars of previous removals.

It may be retouched for possible shaping to fit a mounting.

Flat surface underneath from the original ventricle face of the flake

The end of the scraper usually has an angle of between 70-90°. This makes it efficient in scraping but is not so acute to tear or cut material

Concave end scraper (hollow scraper)
An end scraper on a blade or flake with a concave retouch. These would have been used to smooth wooden shafts

End scraper

Double endscraper

End scraper with a dihedral burin

Rounded ends by retouch

Sides may be used as cutting edges

Held with leather or grass or hafted

Pressure flaking

Flint projectile points and arrowheads

Projectile points appeared in the Middle Palaeolithic, while the leaf points – arrowheads proper – appeared at the beginning of the Neolithic, generally replacing spearheads (although they continued in use). Flint arrowheads continued throughout prehistory, becoming more diverse with time. There are many types and they are widely distributed. Only the basic types are represented here. They are made on blades.

Leaf-shaped/laurel leaf projectile points

A leaf-shaped projectile point is a blade that has been bifacially retouched (i.e. on both sides) and shaped like a leaf. They began in the Upper Palaeolithic when pressure flaking first became common, and would have been hafted to be used as a spear point. Larger versions would probably have been used as knives or daggers. Often they are very thin so would not have been of much practical use. The length varies but could be up to 30cm. They disappear by the late Upper Palaeolithic.

Willow leaf point

Made on blades, they have one or two shoulders and a tang for use with a haft.

At point where the tang meets body there are either one or two shoulders.

Single-edged point

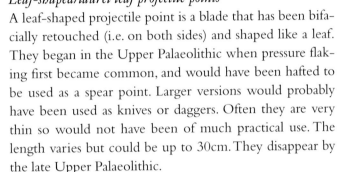

Two retouched edges.
The short side is 60 per cent of the long side.
The base has abrupt retouch.

Tanged Point

The point is thinner than the width of the blade. Tanged points can also be made from sharp flakes requiring no retouch. They first appeared in the Upper Palaeolithic. The tang would be inserted into a haft of bone or wood. Retouch can be on one or both edges of the tang.

75

Barbed and tanged arrowheads

Beginning in the Upper Palaeolithic, barbed and tanged arrowheads continued into the Bronze Age, but were less common in the Mesolithic when microliths took the place of projectile points.

Barb and tangs can be loosely arranged into three types:

1) Small with barb and tangs almost in a horizontal line
2) Barbs developed at the expense of the tang
3) Tang exaggerated in length or breadth with smaller barbs.

Barbs cannot be too big as they would break.

Transverse Point

Transverse points are often made from the middle section of a blade so the cutting edge is the side of the blade.

The cutting edge would leave a wide wound and was probably (rather than used for birds as is often stated) for large, swift animals. The wound made with these wide projectile points would bleed more profusely and thereby slow the animal down.

Transverse points can be loosely arranged into three types: the petit trenchet, chisel and oblique.

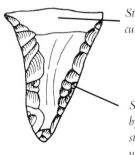

Straight, un-worked cutting edge

Sides blunted by vertical or steep secondary working

Petit tranchet made on flake or blade and smaller than the transverse point. The length is usually at a ratio of 2:1 or greater to the width. Can be broad based, narrow based or have a pointed base

Oblique

Microliths

Despite first appearing in the Upper Palaeolithic, the microlith became most associated with the Mesolithic and was used throughout this period. They are very small worked blades, or bladelets, made on prismatic cores, and were most commonly used in composite tools such as a sickle or harpoon as they were too small to be used by themselves. The cutting edge is left sharp whilst the opposite edge is blunted to fit into a groove in a bone, wood, antler handle. They were quick and easy to make and they were one of the most efficient ways of utilising flint.

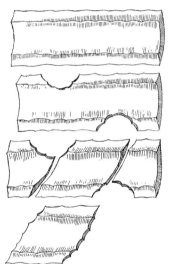

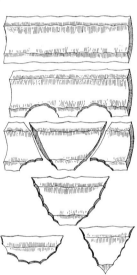

A blank blade

Small notch retouched on side, or sides, of a blade

The ends are snapped off. The ends, the microburins, are waste products and would have been thrown away

The resulting microlith. These can be reworked into different shapes and sizes

Drawings after Bordaz

During the early Mesolithic microliths tended to be large, just over 5cm and simple in form. Obliquely-blunted points are particularly common as well as large isoceles triangles and elongated points with one edge blunted.

In the later Mesolithic a new form of microlits appeared on narrow blades. They were smaller, usually less than 2.5cm long, with a wide range of shapes.

Small blades set in rows in a bone or wooden haft

Gunflints

Flintlock guns were introduced before 1640, but didn't come into general use until the beginning of the eighteenth century. These guns used a square segment of flint fixed into the jaws of the cock which, when fired, would scrape down the 'frizzen' producing sparks which would ignite the gunpowder. This in turn would fire the musket ball. It was necessary to replace the flints often for when a flint got worn the gun misfired. Gunflints were superseded by percussion capsin the 1830s.

The gunflint industry had to produce flints to standardised sizes to fit a variety of guns. Four common types are the pocket pistol, pistol, carbine and musket.

A perfect gunflint flake has a flattish face with even edges. On the dorsal side parallel ribs run the length of the flake but this can only be achieved using high quality flint. More often, the ribs were not parallel and the edges not quite straight. A good flake (approx 15cm long and 2.5cm wide) would produce four gunflints; a very good flake would make five.

Gunflints were produced in many countries but most come from Britain and France. Masses were exported from Britain to America and in the 1850s 11 million were exported from Britain to Turkey alone.

Dorsal

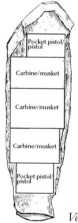

Ventral

   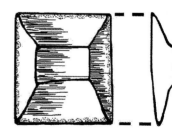

Pocket Pistol   *Pistol*   *Carbine*   *Musket*

Pebble Maceheads

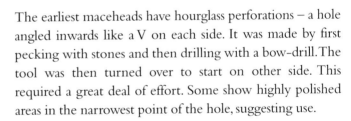

Perforated pebbles, often called maceheads, were used throughout the ancient world. They first appeared in Britain in the late Palaeolithic and lasted until the Bronze Age, so can be difficult to date. However, most date to the Neolithic and, in particular, the Mesolithic. They usually consist of a flattish stone of circular or oblong shape into which a central hole has been drilled. Generally quartzite but other stones are known and it has been suggested that they were used as digging sticks, net-sinkers or weights. Some have battered edges and their use as hammers has been suggested, but rarely is the edge damage so extreme that the shape of the item has been changed. Also the presence of the hole would have weakened the item so it could not have sustained heavy use. The length of time needed to create such items prompted the suggestion that some were of symbolic use and not utilitarian.

There are two types: those with an hourglass hole, and those with a straight hole.

The earliest maceheads have hourglass perforations – a hole angled inwards like a V on each side. It was made by first pecking with stones and then drilling with a bow-drill. The tool was then turned over to start on other side. This required a great deal of effort. Some show highly polished areas in the narrowest point of the hole, suggesting use.

The late Neolithic saw the introduction of a hollow drill bit of wood, bone or antler rotated with a bow. An abrasive such as fine sand would have been used with water to aid the drilling. As a result the hole is cylindrical with straight sides and a cylindrical piece of stone is produced as a by-product. There is less work involved with this method, which is normally associated with the Mesolithic.

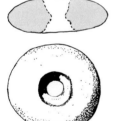

South African rock painting showing a macehead pebble used as a digging stick

Found in a range of sizes, but the average is 6–10cm

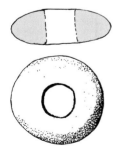

79

Chapter 3
POTTERY

A guide to some pottery forms

Dating pottery can be extremely difficult, even if forms are known. With such a large number of potters working throughout the country there is an enormous variety of quality, shapes and sizes. Distinctions between pots are possible in outputs that may only be twenty miles apart. Also a particular form may be on the decline in one area whilst still very popular in another. Most local pottery will be too bulky and heavy to move so tends to have a limited distribution area. Generally only very high quality pots moved long distances, except for some cheap vessels, such as amphorae, that were used to transport contents. Most periods, however, will exhibit certain overall similarities.

Pottery is usually classified into table, fine and kitchen or coarse ware. Table and fine wares are the ones most likely to be glazed and decorated. Kitchen wares were used for the preparation and storage of food and are generally plain. Kitchen ware often follows a set number of forms but they can have a wide variety of functions.

Bowl

A round, hollow vessel with a height of more than one-third of its width. A hemispherical bowl has a profile resembling half a sphere. A carinated bowl has a sharp change of direction inward often near the centre of its wall, but it can be anywhere on the wall. This may have a practical purpose in retaining dregs when pouring. When there is more than one change of direction the bowl is known as angular.

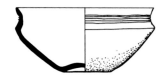

Dish

A shallow vessel, with a height less than one-third but greater than one-seventh of its rim diameter. The rim diameter is always greater than the base diameter. Can have straight, curved or carinated walls.

Ludowici Tg

Plate/Platter

Plates or platters, which appeared in the late Iron Age and were common in the Roman period, have a height no greater than one-seventh of the diameter. They can have straight, curved or carinated walls. After the Roman period true plates disappeared and did not reappear until the post-medieval period.

Dr. 18R

Jar

There is a large variety of jars (both in shape and size), but generally they can be categorised as vessels whose width is less than their height. They can be straight-sided like a bucket or can have constricted necks. The mouth can be either wide or narrow. On a wide-mouthed jar the rim diameter is usually the same, or greater, than the width of the vessel across the shoulder. A fist can normally be placed inside a wide mouth. Narrow-mouthed vessels usually have openings that are less than the width of the vessel across the shoulder.

Jars are often used as cooking pots and they may have soot on their external surface. BB1 jars (those dating from the first century BC to the end of the fourth century, see page 106) are often described as cooking pots. A vase is usually a very ornate jar and an urn is a jar used for funerary purposes.

Beaker

Cup

Tazza

Tankard/Mug

Drinking vessels

There are three general types:

Beakers appear in the late Neolithic onwards and are found in many sizes and shapes. The height is greater than the maximum diameter and they are usually without a handle.

Cups are small, wide, shallow vessels that can be hemispherical or carinated and with or without handles. The rim diameter is always greater than both the base diameter and the height.

Tazzas are a particular type of cup which appeared in prehistoric times where they were often used for incense. The *tazza* is usually in a light-coloured material and distinguished by bands of frilling or pinching, like a pie crust. They often have evidence of burning on the interior.

Tankards or mugs are usually straight-sided vessels with single or double vertical looped handles. The height is greater than the rim, base and maximum diameters. They can be found from prehistoric times onwards and can be very elaborate or simple.

Jugs

Jugs are vessels taller than they are wide, with one or more vertical loop handles, and usually with a lip or spout. They are divided into three forms; *slender*, where the height is at least twice the maximum diameter, *medium* where the height is greater than, but not twice the maximum diameter, and *squat* where the height is less than the maximum diameter.

Pitchers are jugs with shorter necks but this is not a steadfast rule.

Bottles are jugs without handles.

During the Roman period flagons were used in place of jugs.

Slender

Medium   Squat

Rims

There are a number of different types of rim that appear on vessels and these can be diagnostic if only a sherd is present. A few are:

A *simple or plain* rim continues the line of the vessel and is of even thickness.

Simple rim

Hooked rims curve sharply downwards forming a semi-circle.

Hooked rim

Upright rims are roughly vertical.

Upright rim

Everted rims turn sharply out and up from the body and can be in a variety of sizes and shapes, including square, round, pointed and triangular.

Everted rim

A *bead* rim a thickening or turning into protruding bead.

Beaded rim

Flange rims contain a horizontal projection which divides the rim into two halves.

Flanged rim

During the Roman period the *cornice* rim developed, a carefully moulded rim with a steep or undercut profile. This can have a central groove known as a *grooved cornice*, where the rim is divided into two equal ridges.

Grooved cornice rim

Bases

Early Neolithic pottery had sagging bases to facilitate placing the pot on a soft surface. However, late Neolithic pottery such as Fengate is flat-bottomed. From the Iron Age onwards clay may be added to the base to provide a more secure setting.

The *foot-ring* is a ring of clay circling the base on which the pot stands.

A *pedestal base* is an extended foot-ring.

Feet are made from clay and added to the base to form stands.

The base may also have a *kick base* where the body rises upwards to form a hollow dent. In Samian ware the maker's mark is usually on the apex of the rise on the internal floor.

An *omphalos* base has an extra hollow.

Sagging bases can be found on many cooking pots and were designed to prevent cracking both during firing and when used on the fire.

Cutting-off marks

1. Straight parallel lines that indicate the vessel was stationary when it was cut.

2. Curved parallel lines indicate the vessel was rotating slowly.

3. Spiral-pattern indicates the vessel was cut from a rapidly rotating wheel.

Handles

Short, knob-like solid or perforated clay handles that are integral to the body are *lugs* and are common on prehistoric pottery. They are used to suspend the pot. *Looped* handles are made externally and fixed upright to the vessel wall. They are usually curved and can be seen on flagons and jars.

Handles may not be present, and instead the vessel may have a deeply recessed neck or collar to allow for gripping.

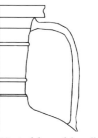

Vertical looped handle

Lugs

Care of Ceramics

Do not immerse unglazed earthenware in water – it will disintegrate.

Do not use a toothbrush on soft earthenware as this will leave marks on the surface and may obliterate any diagnostic information. Use a soft sponge or fingers.

With glazed pieces take care with areas where the glaze has chipped away, or was not present originally, such as foot rims which were often left unglazed.

If copper or iron rivets have been used to repair a piece do not get them wet as they may stain the pottery. Look also for lead plugs which were used to fill cavities.

Prior to the introduction of glazes, prehistoric pots were often burnished with hard objects such as stone, bone or wood to make then more waterproof by closing the pores of clay. Watch for this when washing as burnishing sometimes causes flaking.

Impervious ceramics such as porcelain or bone china can be cleaned in water with a soft brush or cloth. Wash gilding with care to prevent it becoming dislodged. If the vessel has been repaired take care with adhesives as these can be discoloured or weakened by strong light or water. Do not hold any vessel by the edges but place fingers well into the middle. Do not lift anything by a handle but by placing the hands around the whole vessel.

Neolithic Pottery

The first known British pottery appeared in the early to mid-Neolithic. The first forms were bag-shaped, some with lugs on either side of the vessel for suspension over a fire (e.g. Windmill Hill style). The pottery was simply designed, had various local varieties (e.g. Mildenhall style) and had some decoration towards the end of this phase. Often it was burnished with hard objects such as stone, bone or wood whilst still in a leathery state, before firing. After firing, a shiny surface appeared. Watch for this when washing as burnishing sometimes causes flaking. During the Late Neolithic there were fewer regional styles and more uniformity (for example, Ebbsfleet, Mortlake and Fengate) but decoration was extensive. Flat bases appeared and, once established, the bag shape disappeared and vessels became larger.

All Neolithic pottery was handmade, coil built (look for irregular lines on the interior surface, as these can sometimes be seen in the artefact) and black, buff or grey with some red patches due to uneven firing. These are generally known as 'coarse wares'.

Early Neolithic (c.3500-2000 BC)

Plain rims

Lugs (basic handles)

Bag-shaped, based on leather bags, stored in a depression in the ground. No decoration

Windmill Hill style
These were widely traded throughout Britain

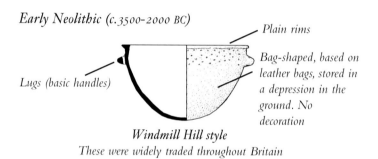

Smooth, burnished surface

If present, simple groove decoration

Mildenhall style

Late Neolithic (c.2000-1500 BC)

Well defined rim

Whipped cord decoration to imitate basketwork. Pottery bearing this type of decoration is collectively termed Peterborough ware

Very thick sides. Early–mid Neolithic walls are thinner than late Neolithic

Mortlake style

Decoration

Decorations are generally lines or geometric shapes such as lozenges. These are generally incised or scratched using wood, stone, finger nails or any other tool.

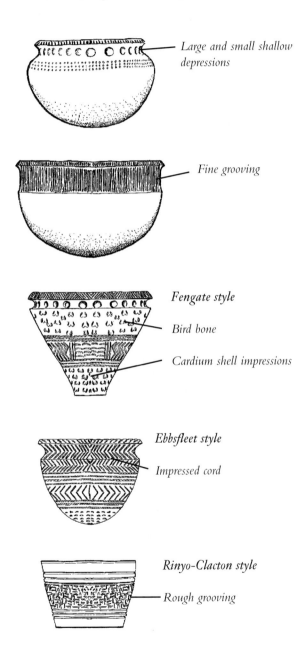

Large and small shallow depressions

Fine grooving

Fengate style

Bird bone

Cardium shell impressions

Ebbsfleet style

Impressed cord

Rinyo-Clacton style

Rough grooving

Bronze Age pottery

Pottery of the Bronze Age was far better developed than that of the Neolithic. The diagnostic vessel, the Beaker (which appeared during the late Neolithic), is thinner and harder and dominated by incised or impressed decorations. Many fragments of Beaker vessels are found but most whole vessels have tended to come from burials.

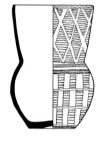

The fabric of beakers is very fine as the temper is a fine sand or well-ground grog (small pieces of crushed pottery added to strengthen the fabric). This is the first time grog is used in pottery fabric. The grog was pre-fired so it was pre-shrunk giving more control over the potting process.

All kinds are oxidised and so are a standard buff colour which occurs over a wide geographic area. Decoration appears in a variety of forms. One of the main types is a series of horizontal lines separating zones. Each zone is filled with a wide variety of grooved motifs (some grooves are burnished). Whipped cord motif is very common and in many cases was probably wrapped around the whole pot and allowed to burn away in the fire. Some grooved ware was inlaid with white paint to emphasise the decoration. During the late Bronze Age decoration decreased and then disappeared.

All beakers are flat bottomed

Middle Bronze Age

During the Middle Bronze Age there was a reduction of types of vessels into one principal form and some secondary ones. The principal form was a collared urn large enough to take the cremated remains of a person and was used extensively for cremations.

The diagnostic feature is a large overhanging collar. Decoration is confined to simple lines on the collar, rarely is there any decoration on the lower half of the vessel.

The quality is so poor that much of late Bronze Age pottery is the worst of all British ceramics. The surface is lightly oxidised with a dark interior where firing has not reached.

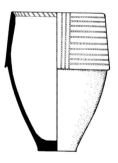

Vessels range in size from 12cm to approximately 1m.

Collard urn

Globular urn

Late Bronze Age

The collard urn was replaced by the bucket urn (which varies in height between 25 and 60cm tall), which loses the collar and becomes a bi-conical vessel.

The whipped cord decoration is still used but not as much as before and it is not so perfectly applied. Many bucket urns have opposing lugs, some pierced horizontally or vertically, and wide mouths which are equal to or less than the height of the vessel. Most urns are of a poor workmanship but they went on to become the dominant vessel in Iron Age.

The collard urn often has a thumbed applied strip or row of thumbed depressions.

During the late Bronze Age, globular urns were very common, had a wide distribution and were made to a high standard. They are wide and rotund, have pierced lugs and are often burnished. The dominant motif is a shallow groove with a variety of patterns, such as horizontal lines, chevrons, deltas and wavy lines.

Iron Age pottery

The standard of Iron Age pottery was far higher than that which had gone before, as the potter's wheel had been introduced *c.*100 BC. The basic periods are Iron Age A (or Hallstatt), B (La Tène) and C (Belgic).

Iron Age A (Hallstatt)

There are two main forms; a large situla or urn and a small omphalos bowl, which differ in both size and quality.

Urns average 45cm high but later in the period they became smaller with less sharp profiles. They then appeared more rounded. with the lower portion more globular – the whole vessel looks more vase-shaped.

Situla urns

Decoration started with a simple thumbing around the base of the neck or grooving around the body. It later developed into large grooves and hatched lozenges, diamonds, triangles and zigzags. At the beginning of the second century BC, stamped patterns, usually a thick, shapeless 'S', occurred. This was the first instance of stamp usage, and occurs mainly in the Welsh Marches and the West Midlands.

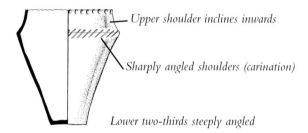

Upper shoulder inclines inwards

Sharply angled shoulders (carination)

Lower two-thirds steeply angled

The walls were thinner than those of Bronze Age pottery and the fabric was usually fully oxidised, so is often red in colour. This is the first time that full oxidisation occurred. The quality varied enormously but generally improved throughout the period.

Omphalos bowls

The bowls generally have a fine temper with the surface lightly burnished. They are on average 10cm high and 25cm in diameter.

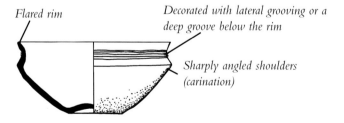

Flared rim

Decorated with lateral grooving or a deep groove below the rim

Sharply angled shoulders (carination)

The base may be flat with an applied foot rim, or flat with kick-up in the base, called an omphalos base

Iron Age B (La Tène)

The most notable development in the La Tène period was the regular use of the wheel, identifiable by smooth regular lines as opposed to the irregular, thick lines of coil built pottery. Vessels were now of a much better quality due also to the use of fine sand as a tempering agent instead of the mixture of shell, flint, etc. that had been used previously. The use of sand produces a more solid body instead of a body broken up by inclusions. The reduction process is also more controlled, resulting in a very black body known as BB ware.

The three principal vessel types are modifications of the situla and omphalos bowl, a large oval jug, a bowl and a small, flat dish. Some areas were very slow to change from Hallstatt to La Tène but, once established, these forms changed very little throughout the next 200 years. By the time of the Romans there were many more forms of which several were to go on through to the Romano-British period.

Jar

The wheel-thrown black burnished jar of varies in size from 15-45cm.

There is intensive burnishing on outside and inside with few decorations except for a central decorated band.

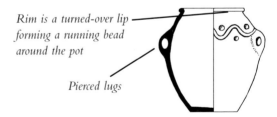

Rim is a turned-over lip forming a running bead around the pot

Pierced lugs

Bowl

Wheel-thrown and black burnished outside and inside.

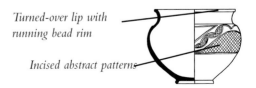

Turned-over lip with running bead rim

Incised abstract patterns

Iron Age C (Belgic)

The fine quality of vessels continues, wheel-thrown and predominantly black, with a wide variety of forms such as large storage jars, globular cooking pots, small bowls and flat turned platters.

Butt beaker
Wheel-thrown and black burnished

Rouletting, or the use of a revolving disc to make a simple, continuous pattern, is introduced

Pedestal urn
Wheel-turned, black burnished

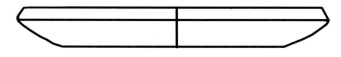

Platters
Platters appear for the first time and are influenced by the Romans, who marked them with potter's stamps. The Belgic imitations also carried potters marks

Roman Samian ware

Samian is the term applied to a red, glossy pottery produced in Gaul and Germany and imported into Britain during the first to third centuries AD. No British Samian was made, with the exception of an imitation ware manufactured in Colchester and distributed across south and east Britain during the second to fourth century; it never attained the same high quality and sheen of Samian. On the Continent Samian ware is generally referred to as *terra sigillata*.

The external appearance of Samian is a smooth, shiny gloss but where chipped it can be seen that the fabric is of a duller and rougher texture. There were a number of potteries producing Samian and therefore the colour, hardness, density and quality of gloss may vary. Also, in later periods the quality of Samian fell as the items were being made more quickly and simply in order to meet demand. Some Samian potters added maker's marks to their vessels; however, the majority of Samian is not marked.

Samian ware has been classified by several people, the best-known series is the Dragendorff, the original series of which runs from numbers 1 to 55. Additional forms were added by Dechelette, Knorr and Walters, and separate type series, to fill in gaps, were added by Ritterling, Curle, Hermet and others. Whenever referring to forms both the name and the number should be used to avoid confusion. Of the main sequence by Dragendorff 1–16 are not commonly found in Britain, 17–30 are generally first-century forms made in southern Gaul and 31–55 are mainly second-century, from central and eastern Gaul.

There are a large number of Samian forms – only some of those found frequently are included here. Samian ware is a luxury ware which may have been curated and passed down through generations, so dates of manufacture may be earlier than the context.

Plate/platter

Dragendorff 15/17, AD 49–c.100

This is a form that would have needed care to make. There are two common types:

Dr. 15/17 almost upright wall, relatively shallow

Dr.15/17

Dr.15/17R Deeper, more flared walls

Dr.15/17r

Dragendorff 18, AD 40–c100

There are two common types:

External offset or step at junction of wall and floor

Footstand triangular in section

Dr. 18 shallow, low, almost upright walls

Beaded lip

Dr.18/31

Stronger external offset or step at junction of wall and floor.

Footstand rectangular/square section

Dr.18

18R spreading walls   *Rouletted circle on floor.*

Dragendorff 18/31, AD 100–160

A form that is a transition between plate and bowl. Two types are most common:

Dr. 18/31 Floor rises steeply to centre

Dr.18/31

Dr. 18/31R Less division between floor and wall but still has slight angle

Squarer and larger footring

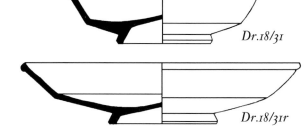

Dr.18/31r

Dishes

Dragendorff 22, AD 40–100

Small, slightly cylindrical dish without a footring.
The wider, shallower version (left) is pre-Flavian
(AD 40–69).

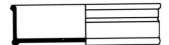

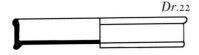

Dragendorff 32, AD 150–250

Often made as a matching set with cup Dr. 40

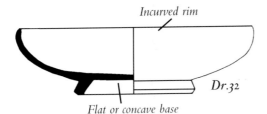

Incurved rim

Plain curved sides with smooth rounded walls

Dr.32

Flat or concave base

Dragendorff 31, AD 140–c.260

Two types most common:

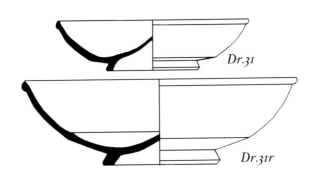

Dr.31

Dr.31r

Dr. 31 Distinction between wall and base still apparent externally. Very deep, almost a bowl. Floor rises very high to the centre with potter's stamp on internal floor

Dr. 31R Wall and base are now a continuous curve, divided by a slight internal ridge. The floor does not reach as high as Dr. 31. Rouletted circle on internal floor

Barbotine is a decorative application using a thick slip that is encrusted on the vessel in patches or trails to form either a picture or pattern.

Dragendorff 36, AD 150–250
Often made as a matching set with cup Dr. 35.

*Overhanging rim ornamented with trailing leaves
en barbotine (thick slip) in form of ivy leaves,
lotus buds on the stem*

Groove internally at the junction of wall and rim

Broad, curved walls

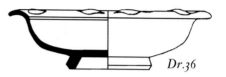

Dr.36

Dragendorff 79, AD 150–250
Often made as a matching set with cup Dr. 80.

*Stronger curved walls and thicker fabric than Dr. 18. May have
rouletted circles on the internal floor*

*Dr. 79 looks like Dr. 18 but has a larger band
on the lip*

Dr.79

*Curle 15 appears during the first century but is
most common in the second century. It is often
made as a matching set with a cup, Curle 46*

Curle 15

Ludowici Tg, AD 150–200
Often made as a matching pair with a cup, Ludowici Tx.

Similar to Dr. 79 but with an upturned rim in form of flange

*May have small step at junction of
wall and floor internally and externally*

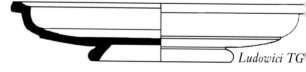

Ludowici TG

Cups
Dragendorff 24/25, 40–c.100

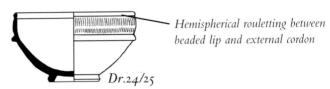

Hemispherical rouletting between beaded lip and external cordon

Dr.24/25

A cordon is a strip of clay on the outside of body for decoration or to help with grip. They may be decorated with finger impressions and there may be more than one cordon.

Dragendorff 27, AD 40–160
This is the the most common cup in the first century but is less so in second century. The second-century versions tend to have a flatter upper wall.

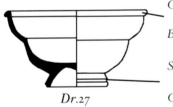

Groove inside, below rounded lip

Beaded rim

Strongly curved double profile with constricted middle

Dr.27

Groove around footstand

Dragendorff 33, AD 70–200
This is the most common cup in the mid- to late second century.

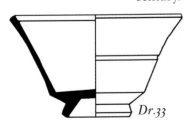

It is conical-shaped with external grooves at the top and bottom of wall. During the second century it has a concave profile, often with a single groove half-way down the outside wall.

Dr.33

Dragendorff 35, *AD 40–200*

Made as a matching pair with dish Dr. *36.*

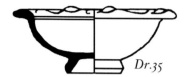

Groove internally at junction of wall and rim

Curved walls with overhanging rim ornamented with training leaves en barbotine

Dr.35

Dragendorff 40, *AD 150–c.260*

Made as a matching pair with dish Dr. *32.*

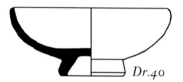

Hemispherical, with an undecorated straight, or slightly curved, flange well below rim. Sometimes gritted to use as a mortarium so may have small spout

Plain curved sides

Footrings may be rounded or chamfered

Dr.40

Dragendorff 80, *AD 150–c200*

Appears as matching pair with dish Dr. *79.*

Dr. *80* can appear like Dr. *27.* The fabric is thicker than *27* but without both present it is difficult for the lay person to distinguish them.

May have rouletted circles on floor

Internal groove below lip

Dr.80

Many of the dishes have a rouletted circle on the internal floor. In addition, most plain Samian ware has a potter's stamp on the internal floor. Stamps tend to follow a standardised form. Some of the most common inscriptions include:

F, Fe, FEC = *fecit* meaning made.
Of, OFIC, OFFIC = *officina* meaning workshop.
M, MA, MAN = *manu* meaning made by hand.

This stamp reads SENNIVSF or 'Sennius made this'

Ritterling 8, AD 60–late first century

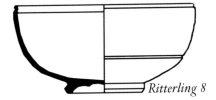

A plain, hemispherical shape

Grooved externally, below lip and second half-way down wall
Fluting inside footring

Ritterling 8

Ritterling 9, AD 60–late first century

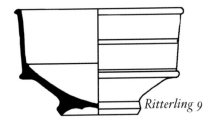

A carinated cup

External groove half-way down wall

Flat or beaded rim matching beaded cordon at join of carination
Footring fluted

Ritterling 9

Curle 46

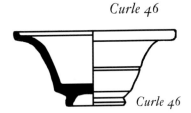

Curle 46 appears in the first century but is most commonly found from the second century

Made as a matching pair with Curle 15
Upturned rim

Curle 46

Ludowici Tx, c.AD 160–third century.
Made as a matching pair with Ludowici Tg. It is similar to Dr. 79 and Dr. 80 but with anupturned rim.

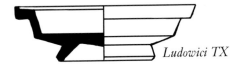

Ludowici TX

Bowls

Dragendorff 38, AD 150–c.260

Rim can be beaded or plain

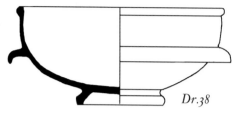

Dr.38

Dragendorff 44, AD 150–c.260

Similar to Dr.38 but has a cordon (horizontal ridge) instead of a flange

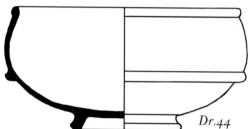

Dr.44

Dragendorff 81, AD 150–c.260
Bowl or wide-mouthed jar.

Upper wall thickens externally, with overhang. Sometimes has potter's stamp on outer wall

Wide neck and slightly everted rim. Rim can be plain, beaded or curved

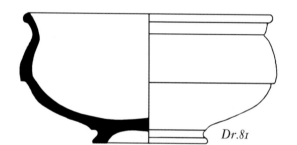

Dr.81

Curle 11
Hemispherical bowl with a flange short way below the rim and decorated with trailed leaves *en barbotine* style.

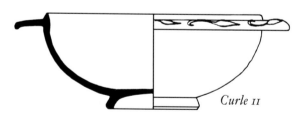

Curle 11

A *straight flange AD 69-79*

B *slightly curved flange AD 70-95*

C & D *further down the bowl, down-turned and hooked flange, second century*

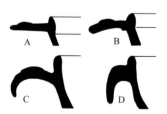

Roman Decorated Samian Ware

Decorated Samian is, in Britain, usually found on carinated, cylindrical and hemispherical bowls. The method of
decoration for 95 per cent of forms was moulding. A stamp
with the decoration was pressed into the interior of a bowl
and then fired to become the mould. A wheel-made bowl
was then pressed into the mould, left until it was leather
hard, removed and fired. Most decorated Samian is dated
by the decoration itself and less by the form, so the following is a rough guide only.

Dragendorff 29, AD 40–100
Carinated bowl.

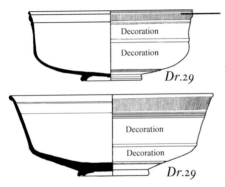

Rouletted rim

*Early forms are more hemispherical, while later
forms (c.AD 80) are more carinated with a
projecting rim*

Dr.29

*Decorated in two zones separated by a narrow
plain cordon where wall becomes carinated. In
early (AD 40) the cordon may be rouletted*

Dr.29   *Footring is often grooved*

Dragendorff 30, AD 40–200
Cylindrical bowl.

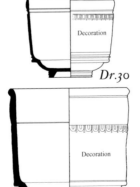

Upper part of the wall is plain

*First-century examples have multiple grooves inside, below
lip; by the second century it has become a single groove*

Dr.30   *Internal grooves level with top of external decoration*

*An egg-and-tongue or, more correctly termed, ovolo design
at top of decoration*

*Decoration covers approximately two-thirds of the wall
surface*

Below the decoration is a curved basal section

Dr.30   *The footring is pad-like*

Dragendorff 37, AD 65–c.250

Hemispherical bowl. There is a plain band below a beaded lip. Early forms (c.AD 70) have a narrower plain zone above the decoration than those in the second century. Late forms can have a very large plain zone. If sherds from this part of the vessel are found it may not be obvious that they are from a decorated form.

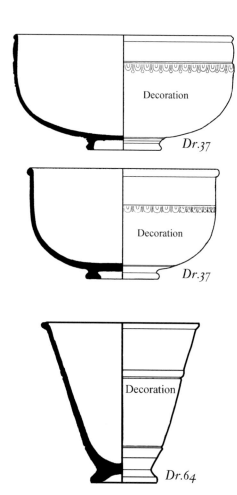

Interior is plain

Ovolo design at top of decoration

In the second century forms of the decoration can be divided by vertical and horizontal lines into panels. These can have figures scattered over the whole surface, and hunting scenes are common

The footstand is pad-like

Dragendorff 64, AD 100–150
Conical beaker.

Plain band below beaded rim

Decoration bounded by plain cordons

Plain band below decoration

The footring is splayed

Dragendorff 67, AD 70–140
Globular beaker.

Everted rim

Upper zone plain

Decoration usually bounded by two or more grooves.

Solid base

Dragendorff 68, AD 120–200
Jar.

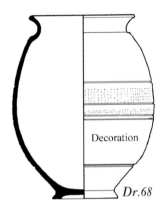

Sometimes has black slip

Defined shoulder with curved rim

Central band of rouletting

Decorated zone lower half of wall with plain band below

Splayed footstand

Dragendorff 72, AD 100–150
Globular beaker.

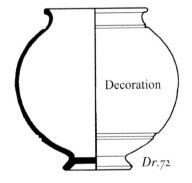

Neck curved with beaded rim

Decorated zone covers most of wall bounded by grooves above and below

Plain band above footstand

The footstand is splayed

Dragendorff 78, AD 70–c.150
Small carinated bowl.

Straight sides which slope outwards from the base

Sometimes has ovolo above the decoration

Plain band below carination

Does not have footstand

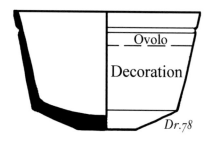

Black Burnished ware

A coarse ware, primarily for kitchen ware, consisting of everted-rim jars, flat-rimmed bowls and plain dishes. Made in Britain, they can be divided into two types: Black Burnished ware 1 (BB1) and Black Burnished ware 2 (BB2).

BB1 (first century BC–end of fourth century)

This appeared in the late Iron Age, primarily in the Dorset region, and was always handmade. The fabric is dark grey or black, gritty and coarse with noticeable inclusions. There are a large number of forms.

During the first and second centuries the exterior was highly burnished or smoothed. During the third and fourth centuries the exterior was slipped (the slip can be difficult to distinguish but sometimes drip marks are visible) and burnished. Burnishing may appear all over the vessel or on the shoulders, necks and rims only and internally on the rims.

Only the exterior walls on jars are burnished. On open vessels such as bowls and dishes the interior is also burnished.

Decoration consists of zones of latticed lines (to provide a better grip) which form three types:

Acute Lattice (AD 120–160): where the angle of the lines to the horizontal is greater than 45°.

Square Lattice (AD 160–280): where the intersecting patterns form a distinct square.

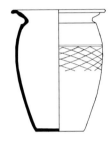

Obtuse Lattice (AD 280–370): where the angle of the lines to the horizontal is less than 45°. As the obtuse lattice becomes more dominant the zone of decoration narrows and decreases from approximately 50 per cent of the wall to 25 per cent.

In fourth-century examples, a line is common above the lattice panel. A burnished wavy line on the neck may be present on early mid-second-century vessels. They may have everted, or beaded, rims. Necks are countersunk to provide a means of gripping. The profile is globular with flat base.

The body becomes more slender and narrower in proportion to the mouth. The early vertical rim becomes more splayed and flared and by the end of the period the rim is greater than the width of the body.

BB2 *(AD 120–fourth century)*
BB2 vessels share many of the same forms as BB1 but they are now wheel-thrown. The fabric is hard and ranges from a dark grey or black to brown or reddish-brown. The burnished surface has a much silkier feel than BB1.

Roman Fine Ware beakers/cups

Apart from Samian ware, Roman pottery also included other fine wares. Many of these were made at the same workshops as Samian and use the same fabrics, but are coated with a dark-coloured slip. These are generally known as colour-coated wares. However, many other fine wares, although sharing the same forms as Samian, are differentiated by their fabric and decoration. The principal kind of colour-coated ware is the drinking vessel, often identified by decorations of vine leaves and grapes. Other forms were also produced including flagons, bowls, plates, dishes and beakers. All are dark-slipped, roughcast or barbotine decorated. Hardly any carry maker's marks. Made from the first to the fourth century, beakers were particularly popular in the third and fourth centuries.

High shouldered beakers were made from AD 40 to the third century but were particularly popular in the first century. They have a narrow mouth and base, with high shoulders and a globular profile, and were often decorated with fine sand called roughcast. Taller than they are wide, they average 15–20cm high.

Bag-shaped beakers were made from AD 50–third century but particularly popular in the late first and second centuries. They have a wide mouth with straight walls that flare out below the rim and then turn in sharply towards the base at a distance approximately one third of the length of the vessel. Early types have cornice rims, but later (third century) they have plain rims. Taller than they are wide, they average 15–20cm high. There are a number of types of decoration; the most common are roughcast or decorated in barbotine, rouletting and white painting. Scenes are often of hunting, showing animals, usually dogs, chasing hares or deer, these are referred to as 'hunt-cups'. Gladiator scenes were produced from AD 150-250.

Decoration

Indented, or folded, beakers were made from the second to third centuries. They have evenly spaced indented, or hollow, sides. Seven and nine indentations are common. Indented beakers were often used for playing dice.

They can be decorated in a variety of ways, including roughcast, barbotine and white painted. Taller than they are wide, they average 15–20cm high.

Cups, *AD* 40-70

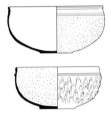

Small, wide, shallow, hemispherical cups were more popular than beakers. They are decorated with roughcast and applied pointed scales. Other decoration includes rustication, or the lifting of the body wall to create ridges and designs.

Roman mortaria

Mortaria are large, thick, hemispherical or conical strong vessels used for mixing food. They do not appear before the Roman period or after. Initially they were imported from the Rhineland but soon after the Conquest they were being made in Britain. Mortaria are classified according to the Dressel system.

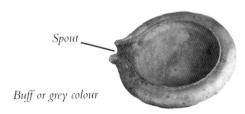

Spout

Buff or grey colour

Coarse grit of quartz or other resilient stone is embedded in internal surface to use for grinding. Often mortaria are recovered quite worn with hardly any grit left, showing long use

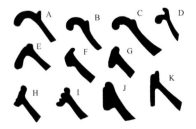

Very distinct rims for easy gripping

Rims vary considerably from early wall-sided to later curved and hooked

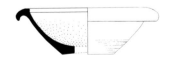

Stamps usually representing the maker appear on British mortaria during the first and second centuries. They are the only Romano-British vessels that carry stamps; all other stamps on Roman ware are on imports. Mortarium stamps are usually found on the rims, sometimes decorated with borders of herring bone pattern, and sometimes reversed. There is a corpus of names known which can be used to trace the career of a potter and how either he, or his mortaria, moved around the country. These marks have provided a large number of Celtic names that are not known from any other source.

A distinctive Samian mortarium from the second century is distinguished by the presence of a lion's head spout around which are a number of radiating lines. The spout consists of a hole in the lion's mouth. Often the mould was so reused that the image begins to look more like a bat than a lion.

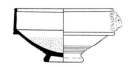

The walls of the mortaria are also distinctive in that they are straight and wall-like.

Roman Flagons

Flagons were used to hold liquids, particularly wine, and generally consist of a globular body with one or more handles, a tall narrow neck and a height of up to 37cm. Few flagons have spouts. They are often of a creamy coloured fabric with no decoration and have a variety of neck types such as ring-, flange-, disc- or screw-neck.

Ring-neck flagon
A very common type, AD 70–200.

In the mid-first century the neck is more or less vertical to body

Slightly flaring 'trumpet' mouth

Series of three, four or five conjoined rings

Globular body

Footring

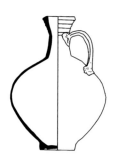

The handle goes from below the rings to the shoulder. The earliest handles are bent almost at right angles, are broad, flat and can have two, three or four ribs

Around AD *120-200* the number of rings decreases with the top ring becoming splayed outwards and protruding over the other rings.

The handle becomes smaller.

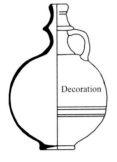

Decoration

Flange-neck flagon, c.AD 240–fourth century

By the fourth century the neck is narrow with two flanges divided by a pronounced collar that is level with the top of the handle. It may have decoration on the central zone of the wall.

Hofheim flagon

The Hofheim flagon is common in Britain from c.AD 43-70.

This single- and doubled-handled flagon has a cylindrical neck with a distinctive rim with out-curved lips that are triangular in section. The handles are square in section.

Roman amphorae

An amphora is a tall ceramic urn with a long cylindrical neck, large handles on each side and a body tapering to a point. They are normally an unglazed grey or yellow/buff in colour, and are made on a wheel with the handles moulded on separately. The base has a thin projection upon which it balances and it could be rotated on this point to move, rather than bodily lifting the vessel. The shape was intended for ease in stacking and handling and generally the height was between 50-77cm. The content could be poured by holding the bottom point and one of the handles.

They were used extensively throughout the Roman period for storage (thick earthenware maintains a cool temperature) and for shipping. Many amphora studies have looked at examples recovered from wrecks. They contained wine, olive oil, fish paste and many other commodities. The Greek amphora, upon which the Roman amphora was based, held about 39 litres; the Roman amphora was smaller and carried about 26 litres. Amphorae were often recycled: they could be utilised as storage vessels in a house or elsewhere as well as cremation burials for the poor.

There is a wide variety of amphora types and often countries have different, ever increasing, typologies for local ware. However, amphora types, dates and places of manufacture were first classified by Heinrich Dressel in Germany in 1899 and it is by his classification that many forms are still known. Many Dressel forms are not found in Britain, so only those basic types that have a regular presence in this country have been included.

Dressel Type 1

Originating in Italy in the late second century to the early first century the earliest type is a tall cylindrical amphora. It has a wide distribution around the Mediterranean and the north-west provinces of the Roman Empire. Many examples have been recovered from shipwrecks. Dressel 1 appears in Britain before the Conquest and carried mainly wine but also oil, and would have had a capacity of approximately 24 litres. There are two basic types: Dressel 1A and Dressel 1B.

Dr1A. *second century BC. More common in the south-west, rarer in south-east and differ from 1B in that they have a triangular rim*
Dr1B. *c.50-10 BC*

Mouths were quite small and would have been sealed with a bung. The rim has a distinctive collar

Long-waisted neck

Angled shoulders

Long, straight handles generally oval in section

Long, slightly flared, spike

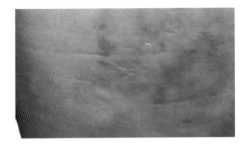

Wheel lines can often be seen on the outside of the vessel

Amphora sherds can be mistaken for building material. Look for wheel lines both internally and externally

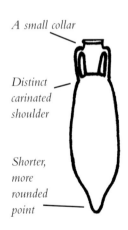

©PAS

Dressel Types 2–4

Similar to Dressel 1, types 2–4 are the most widely produced amphora types. They are very varied but generally are a tall cylindrical amphora with long bifid handles composed of two rods.

Production continued from the later first century BC through to the end of the first century AD, and probably beyond. They have been found in pre-Conquest deposits in Britain, but are most common on early Roman sites.

They were used principally for wine, but occasionally fish-based sauces, olive-oil and dates.

This is the most important wine amphora of the early imperial period, and was exported widely throughout the Continent.

A shorter, straighter, neck than Dressel 1 so capacity increases to approximately 34 litres

Occasionally stamped near the base, or on the neck or handle

A small collar

Distinct carinated shoulder

Shorter, more rounded point

Dressel Types 7–11

Produced in southern Spain and exported widely during the first and second centuries AD. These types have bulbous bodies with, in 7 and 8, a tapered base reaching up to one-third of the total length of the vessel.

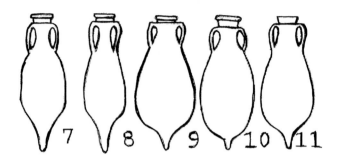

Dressel types 7-11 were mainly used mainly for fish products

Dressel type 20

This amphora is widespread on early sites from the beginning of the first century to *c.*AD 260. One of the largest amphorae, it had a capacity of approximately 80 litres and was imported from southern Spain.

Prominent beaded or thickened, rounded or angular rim

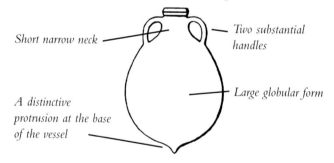

Short narrow neck

Two substantial handles

Large globular form

A distinctive protrusion at the base of the vessel

Dressel Type 43

The most notable feature of this type is the high peaked handles.

Stamps

Stamps are often included on the rim or neck, generally as a small square or rectangle with one or two letters or symbols. Stamps can be used to trace a particular workshop or production area and to date the vessel.

Painted inscriptions usually indicate the contents and are usually faint and may only be visible under certain lights, but their presence should be kept in mind when cleaning. Over 40 inscriptions are known and can be referenced in Collingwood's seminal work on stamps (see bibliography).

Anglo-Saxon pottery

Anglo-Saxon mercenaries arrived in Britain during the second half of the fourth century/first half of fifth. Much of their wares are defined by fabric types. However, there are two basic types: domestic and funerary.

Romano-Saxon

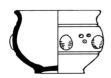

Pot with bosses

Cooking pot

Knife marks

After the departure of the Romans there was a break in pottery forms. Although some makers did use Roman forms they are decorated in the Anglo-Saxon style using bosses, dimples and free linear ornament. Wheel-thrown, mass-produced pottery gave way to handmade ware.

Domestic pottery is difficult to date: much of it consists of very simple, undecorated, small, globular cooking-pots which remained unchanged over a long time and, despite the generic name, were used for a variety of functions. Much Anglo-Saxon domestic pottery can be confused with Iron Age pottery, but it tends to be more finely grained with few grits, fired quite hard, with colours from brown, grey and black; it may show signs of being coil-built. Much of it has burnished surfaces. Many have sagging bases that have been shaped by a knife, and knife marks may be visible.

During the Middle Saxon period (c.650–850) cooking pots have upright pierced lugs which are characteristic of this period.

Early and mid-Saxon pottery was made on a slow wheel, one that was revolved by hand. As there was no mechanical means to generate sufficient momentum the wall of the pots tends to be thicker than in later examples, when a mechanical wheel was used. Wheel-thrown pottery results in thinner walls.

Funerary vessels are predominantly 'urns' that held cremated human remains. More care was taken in the construction of funerary urns than with domestic pottery. Funerary vessels can be difficult to date, particularly plain urns, and, as they have been used in cremation, they can be distorted and difficult to identify. Funerary pottery is usually dated by the manner of its ornamentation, which may be linear, boss or stamp. The earliest kind is simple linear patterns.

As with domestic pottery, later funerary urns have thinner walls as a result of being wheel-thrown.

Linear decoration may be horizontal, biconical or curvilinear. Early decoration consists of chevron patterns and standing arched grooves.

Bosses appear very early in Anglo-Saxon pottery, in the fifth century. The early examples are simple, expanding to long bosses, and finally culminate in the highly decorated *Buckelurnen*. By the sixth century bosses waned in popularity and the use of stamps increased.

Stamps The early use of stamps was in conjunction with bosses. However, by the end of the sixth century stamps were the dominant form of decoration. The stamps were generally made of wood and can include simple crosses, circles, squares and triangular shapes. They can also feature include animals and swastikas.

Funerary urns are not found from the seventh century onwards due to spread of Christianity.

Linear

Bosses

Long bosses

Buckelurnen

Stamps

Medieval pottery

There is a large range of medieval pottery with some 70 forms registered, many of which are difficult to date. All these pots, however, are based on three common, wheel-thrown forms: jugs, jars and bowls. Within these three forms is a wide range of variations and functions. Cups are not common, as wooden bowls were more popular and plates tended to be trenchers, wooden blocks or slabs of stale bread. Plates proper did not return until the post-medieval period. Also, a number of metal vessels were being produced, such as pewter (see page 27), to replace pottery.

From the twelfth century there was also much imported pottery, particularly from France, including polychrome jugs and pitchers.

The three forms of medieval pottery:

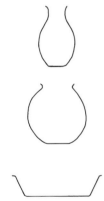

Jugs: Tall, closed wares where the diameter of the opening and the maximum width are less than the height.

Jars: Closed wares with a width approximately the same as the height. The diameter of the opening is usually less than the width or the height.

Bowls: Open wares where the diameter of the rim is more than either the width or the height.

Glazes

Medieval pottery has characteristic glazes that were introduced at the beginning of the twelfth century when lead glazes, particularly on jugs, began to be used. It was not until the thirteenth century that glazes also became common on cooking vessels. Early glazes were applied in the form of a dry powder which produced a characteristic dull, spotted and pitted appearance. Glazes were usually applied to the upper half of a vessel – sometimes liberally, sometimes sparsely.

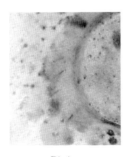

Pitting

In the late twelfth and early thirteenth centuries, a liquid glaze was used, either by painting or dipping a pot; this resulted in a more even appearance with a high gloss. In the late fifteenth and early sixteenth centuries the thick, mottled, dark green glaze commonly referred to as 'Tudor green' was widely used.

Medieval pots were fired once, the glaze being put on the unfired vessel. Not until the seventeenth century, when biscuit firing came in, were pots fired, glazed and fired again.

Jugs

Jugs come in a wide range of sizes and shapes and range from crudely made to highly decorated. Smaller jugs tend to be plain, the larger ones more decorated. More elaborate forms are the distinctive vessels in the shapes of humans or animals or the aquamaniles. Some of the more common examples are the face jugs of the fourteenth and fifteenth centuries, with a bearded face at the top of the vessel, and sometimes having arms. Others include the knight jugs, spouted and highly decorated with horses and knights. Puzzle jugs were designed to tease the pourer. Many of these would have been used for pouring water over the hands before a meal.

In the fourteenth century drinking jugs replaced wooden bowls. These can be crudely made, orangeish or a creamy off-white in colour, with only a few splashes of glaze, and roughly finished. The handles are simple and attached by rough thumb impression and the base may have a crinkled effect created by thumb impressions. These small jugs could also have ful-filled a wide range of purposes from sauce pots to urinals. In the late fourteenth and fifteenth centuries metal ware began to replace pottery table wares and small jugs become scarcer.

Scars and marks on medieval jugs are quite common. Vessels were usually fired upside-down and the flow of the glaze can often be seen. As they were placed close together in the kiln they became stuck and, when prized apart, would leave scars and marks. It was not until the early fifteenth century that saggers (clay pieces to keep vessels apart) were used.

Jars

The classification of jars includes a number of related forms such as cooking pots, pipkins and cauldrons.

The cooking pots range from small ones, holding approximately 3–5 pints to large, with a capacity of 1.5–2.5 gallons. Many, despite being classified as cooking pots, would have been used for storage; certainly the large would have been difficult to move around, especially when full. Those that were used for cooking are distinguished by a blackened, sooty exterior. However, they were never placed directly into the fire but rather on hot embers, on a trivet over the fire or suspended over the fire. Medieval Cornish ware has suspension lugs for this purpose. By the mid-fourteenth century, cooking pots diminished in popularity in some areas as ceramic pipkins increased.

Pipkins

Pipkins appeared during the twelfth and thirteenth centuries. Some have a blackened exterior showing they were used over a fire, but they could also have been used for serving or preparing food. Later examples have three feet. By the mid-fourteenth century there was a shift from using large cooking pots to pipkins.

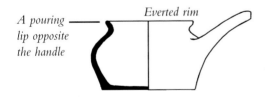

A pouring lip opposite the handle

Everted rim

Straight handle attached either to the rim or the body

Small, rounded, cooking pot shape

Cauldron

A double-handled jar with three feet and two opposing vertical loop handles. However, there are variations to this.

Bunghole/cistern jars

Ale was an important drink in medieval times and from the fourteenth century when brewing beer became common, bungholes/cisterns were used for pouring liquids .

They are large jars with vertical loop handles and a bunghole near the base to allow liquids to be drawn off, leaving the sediment on the base. The bunghole can either be a piercing in the body or a circular piece of clay added to the body. They usually had a wooden tap and the top of the jar would be covered, probably with cloth.

Bowls

Bowls would have been used for food preparation, particularly dairy, pastry and bread products, for eating from or even washing clothes in. There is a wide range of sizes and shapes and they sometimes have handles and feet. Some allied forms of bowls are skillets and dipping dishes.

Skillets

Generally used for frying, these are spouted bowls with a similarity to pipkins. However, skillets are broader and shallower, with the rim diameter large than base diameter. They can have straight handles and occasionally have feet.

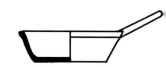

Dipping dishes

Dipping dishes or dripping pans, also called fish dishes, were usually placed beneath a roast to catch the fat. Often they are blackened on one side, mainly opposite the handle, where they were placed in the hot embers. They are fairly shallow and could vary in shape – they could be oval or rectangular.

Earthenware

Earthenware (prehistoric earthenware is called coarse ware in archaeology) is the most common form of ceramic. It has been made worldwide since ancient times (the earliest pottery in Britain is Neolithic) and continues to be hand-made today in such as Central and South America and Africa, following ancient techniques that have changed little. It is also used in contempory ceramic wares. Most of our modern dinner services are glazed earthenware, and only the manufacturing methods have changed.

Earthenwares are split into many different types, but the main groups covered here are: earthenware, lead glazed and tin glazed.

Prehistoric earthenware

Prehistoric pottery is handmade. Handmade vessels are constructed by winding coils of clay on top of each other. Therefore, look for irregular lines, usually on the interior of the vessel. In fact, coil pottery continued to be produced until the twelfth century and can be confused with prehistoric pottery.

Exterior colour

Exterior surface colours are black, brown, buff, red, white or grey depending on the clay and mineral inclusions. Any red patches visible may be due to uneven firing. Many medieval earthenwares are also black or dark brown because they were fired in a sealed kiln where oxygen is limited. Most post-medieval earthenwares are red because they tend to have been fired in a kiln with plenty of oxygen.

Internal colour

Early earthenware often has an interior core of a dark grey or black. This is due to the firing temperature not being high enough to fully heat the interior. This type of low firing can be found right up until medieval times.

Wheel-made pottery

Wheel-made pottery has evenly spaced lines and dates at the earliest to the first century BC, when it was being imported from the Roman world. However, after the Romans the art of making pottery on a wheel was lost, and Anglo-Saxon pottery can resemble that of the Iron Age.

Wheel-thrown pottery usually has a flat base, with concentric rings where the pot was cut from the table.

Temper

Earthenware is usually made from common, or secondary, clays, i.e. clays that have moved from their place of formation and later been contaminated with minerals, etc. Common clays are too sticky to be used alone, so are tempered with sand, flint, shells and other materials. The mixture is then fired at a 'low' or 'bonfire' temperature, usually below 2,200°F (1,200°C). At this temperature the clay cannot vitrify, or fuse together, so the pot remains porous and unable to hold liquids.

Prehistoric fabric is tempered with eggshell, shells, flint, quartz, and other materials, and the pottery appears very coarse with large inclusions.

Modern earthenware bodies are fine-grained and impervious, but the glaze sits 'on' the body.

Stoneware

Stoneware was first produced at the end of fourteenth century, when it was developed in the Rhineland, Germany. It became very popular during the fifteenth century and most examples come from Germany. England began to produce stoneware in 1671. Stoneware came to be preferred for domestic use, not only for its durability but also for keeping things cool in storage. It declined in popularity due to the demand for creamware (see page 127).

It differs from earthenware in several ways, most noticeably in that it is impervious; even if left unglazed it is hard and durable. Stoneware is fired at a high temperature – 2,250°F (1,400°C) – so that it vitrifies into a non-porous body. It can also be thinly potted, which sometimes makes it translucent, so it may be mistaken for porcelain. Most stoneware vessels are salt-glazed, a medium achieved by throwing common rock salt into the kiln at approximately 1,800°F (1,000°C) during firing. Enamel colours became popular after 1745. Body texture ranges from rough to smooth and body width from thick to thin.

Colours range from dark buff or brown and reddish/orange to light or whitish colours, which were made from the eighteenth century onwards.

To many people stoneware is most familiar as Victorian ink bottles, ginger beer bottles and as sewer pipes.

Salt-glazed stoneware is probably most popularly known in the form of the bellarmine jar. It has the 'orange-peel' look with a slightly rough texture. Bellarmines date from c.1520-40 to the 1760s The popular legend has it that the face was modelled on the unpopular Cardinal Bellarmine as an expression of contempt. However, face mugs had already been used for years previously. The term 'ugly mug' is taken from these kinds of vessels.

Bellarmines vary between 10cm and about 55cm in height and were used mainly in taverns to carry the wine to the table. Smaller versions were probably drinking mugs.

On the base are concentric circles or grooves (see page 86). These generally start at a fixed point on the edge of the base and extend across the base of the vessel. Twisted wire or cord was used to cut the vessel from the wheel; some were thumbed smooth afterwards.

The mask is one third as long as vessel.

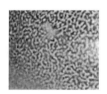

Orange-peel appearance

The body is one, the glaze is not visible

In Germany from around 1587 a bright cobalt-blue salt glaze was used on a light-coloured stoneware, resulting in a ware called Westerwald. The most common form found is a jug with white relief moulding. After 1665 sometimes a manganese purple colour is used.

Westerwald

From the late thirteenth to the fifteenth century, stoneware mugs and jugs from Germany were imported by their thousands. They are unglazed, an off-white colour with rare examples of decoration. Nearly all have a distinctive frilled, pinched base.

In around 1720, a white, salt-glaze stoneware was developed in Britain by adding white Devonshire clay and powdered flint. White stoneware mugs decorated with scenes became popular in the eighteenth century. They are often glazed on the upper half.

White stoneware

White salt-glaze was used extensively for kitchen ware as it can keep contents cool, is easy to clean and cheap to make. These vessels are impervious, have a matt appearance and were made extensively, often quite crudely, as marmalade jars, toothpaste pots and mustard pots, to name but a few kinds of vessel.

Earlier stoneware bottles had the manufacturer's name and contents etched onto them, but by the mid-nineteenth century transfer printing or decorative underglazing was used.

White stoneware toothpaste pot lid

Thousands of ink wells in stoneware were made during the Victorian, and later, times and can be found in any boot sale quite cheaply. Production of stoneware vessels for the supply of various liquids continued until the 1960s.

The stoneware fabric is a rough white often glazed with a white lead glaze

Tin-glazed earthenware

Tin-glazed pottery resulted from the race to imitate Chinese porcelain and became known for its stylised Chinese decorations in blue and white. It became very popular as it could be made locally and was seen as a cheap substitute for porcelain.

Tin glaze was made the in the same way worldwide: namely an earthenware base was given a lead glaze and then a tin oxide glaze, which gave the vessel an opaque white finish. This smooth surface made it possible to add decoration. It is called Maiolica in Italy, Delft in the Netherlands (Dutch delft is spelt with a capital D), delftware in England (English delftware is spelt with a lowercase d) and faience in France and Germany. Tin glaze is less easily fused than lead glaze, and so does not run or blur in the kiln so much.

Tin-glazed ware was not strong enough for daily use; the tradition of adding milk to tea began with tin glaze. Milk lowered the temperature of the water and prevented the cup from cracking.

Tin-glazed ware dates from the mid-sixteenth to late eighteenth centuries, when it was phased out in favour of creamware (see page 127).

The body is soft, very porous, and easily damaged. It tends to chip and crack badly so that the surface glaze breaks up, causing *crazing*, a fine series of lines, when the glaze contracts more under firing than the body.

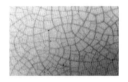

Crazing

Tin glaze was very common in Europe, especially for apothecaries' jars. The peak of British delft was during the mid-eighteenth century, and manufacture sharply declined thereafter.

Tin glaze reflects light, so decorations will appear more brilliant than those on lead glazes.

Pitting

Pitting is common as air escapes in the kiln. Spots range from large to small.

The glaze sits on top of the body (left).

If a 'stilt' is present on the base, it was caused by a piece of clay on which the vessel rested in the kiln to keep it apart from its neighbours. It dates roughly to the late seventeenth or eighteenth centuries.

When blue-and-white lost popularity Dutch Delft produced bright colours.

Maiolica: this term applies to Italian tin-glazed earthenware which was produced from the fifteenth century and on into the eighteenth.

Lead-glazed earthenwares

To protect earthenware vessels and to make them more waterproof, glazes were added to the surface of the vessel. These provided either a translucent or opaque (coloured or white) surface, but were not generally common before the late twelfth century. Lead glaze is a glassy glaze often found on both Chinese and European earthenware and was in use from the second century AD. These glazes are prone to 'breaking down' over time, which can produce an iridescent effect on antique pieces. Lead glazes are easily scratched.

Slipware, *c.*1680–1800

Applied with spouted vessel or quill or dropped from brush, dotted or trailed with brush.

The slip-trailing after firing often stands proud from the body and can be felt with the fingers. A technique revived in modern times by potters such as Bernard Leach.

Mainly popular during the seventeenth and early eighteenth centuries, slipware takes its name from the method of applying trails of slip (clay mixed with water to make it easy to apply) to a fired earthenware body to produce a picture or pattern. Alternatively, the body was dipped in a tinted lead glaze, usually yellow but sometimes brown, copper or green, and fired. The slip was then cut away to a design or picture, revealing the contrasting earthenware

(often red or buff) underneath. This technique is known as sgraffito and had a revival in the twentieth century under potters like Michael Cardew.

In Tudor times the bulk of domestic English pottery was lead-glazed. Adding copper oxide resulted in the typical 'Tudor Green' characteristic with uneven smears (see page 118).

Creamware, c.1761–1846
Renamed Queen's Ware in 1765

A transfer-printed plate with openwork piercing – a Leeds speciality.

Creamware is yellow- or butter-coloured opaque glaze originating in the 1760s. It was tough enough for everyday use, light in weight and inexpensive, and it replaced the heavier, more fragile, tin-glaze delftware in the late eighteenth century.

By 1775 creamware had spread to the Continent and was exported widely. Its heyday in the 1760s–70s saw a great deal being produced and so it is regularly found today.

It was at about this time that uniform dinner services were being produced instead of the haphazard collection of wares. From around 1760, transferware, or the application of a picture transfer, can found on creamware.

Pearlware

This was fine, sometimes thinly potted earthenware (similar to creamware), developed in England, by Wedgwood. Pearlware is characterised by a faint bluish-white tint to its glaze; this is most evident in crevices where the glaze pools. It was an improvement on creamware and closer in appearance to porcelain, but was cheaper.

Majolica: this differs from the Italian Maiolica, as it is a nineteenth-century earthenware developed by Thomas Minton and is characterised by moulded decoration and richly coloured lead glazes.

Porcelain

Porcelain was a Chinese invention (from the Han dynasty, 206 BC–AD 220) which came to be greatly admired and desired by the West. For years Europeans tried to discover the secret of porcelain but were unable to imitate it. The nearest they came was soft paste porcelain until the late eighteenth century, when they were able to make hard paste, or 'true' porcelain. Also in the eighteenth century another form of porcelain unique to Britain was developed: bone china.

Soft paste, *c.*1738-1800s

The ingredients of soft paste lack the kaolin found in hard paste so it does not vitrify and remains soft. Early soft paste was too fragile for utilitarian pieces so was mainly confined to figurines and ornamental ware. When it was used for utilitarian pieces it gave rise to a few traditions; teapots would crack if boiling water was placed in a cold pot so the pot was warmed first and drinking from a saucer was considered acceptable as the water would be cooler. Adding milk to tea had already become customary with tin plate pottery.

The body is soft and granular like sand and not as durable as hard paste. Damaged edges look like the texture of a sugar cube; chips look floury and are rough to the touch.

The surface is vulnerable to scratching and pitting. The base can look 'bubbly'.

The body is often creamy, or a greyish/off-white in tone rather than the white of hard-paste porcelain. It is warmer and softer to the touch than the colder hard-paste. When held up to the light it is not as transparent as hard paste.

It is more porous than hard-paste and unglazed parts may be discoloured. The glaze tends to be thick and pools in crevices. It can be easily scratched.

Soft paste, like tin glaze (see page 125), develops surface cracks, particularly when immersed in, or containing hot liquids.

Crazing or crackling is found on some soft paste porcelains but not on hard paste porcelain.

When gilding is present, it is soft, warm and not metallic-looking. The glaze sits on the surface like a glassy layer.

Colours are softer and delicate as the body is more porous; they therefore merge with the glaze.

Less glittery than hard past.

The glaze may be imperfect and have black specks.

Also, is is susceptible to corrosion by citric acid so cannot be used for storing fruit.

Hard paste, or 'true' porcelain, 1770s–1812

The difficulty in imitating true porcelain came from a lack of the essential ingredient kaolin, or china clay. In the late eighteenth century it was found in Cornwall, where it is still mined today. The other ingredient of hard paste or true porcelain is petuntse, like kaolin a form of granite and only found in China. The ingredients are then fired at high temperatures – 2,280°F (1,250°C) to 2,640°F (1,450°C). These new ingredients allowed for a greater innovation in decoration and colours than with soft paste. Because it is the hardest and most durable ceramic product, porcelain is used for electrical insulators and laboratory equipment.

The body and glaze fuse together, making one body so a separate glaze cannot be distinguished either in breaks or on chips. Porcelain is extremely tough, it withstands heat and boiling water and is very durable. The body is usually thin and impervious to liquids. It has the appearance of smooth glass and is slightly translucent, so will let bright light through.

If fine porcelain is held up to light and a hand or finger placed between the light and the piece, a shadowy outline should be visible. Pottery, with the exception of some stoneware, will not allow light through. However, some thicker porcelains can be opaque.

The body colour varies from pure white to cream, depending on the ingredients but generally is glittery and shines in the light. The body surface will be smooth like icing with fewer scratches and discolouring. It is colder and harder to the touch than soft paste.

Colours are harsher and less delicate than on soft paste and when gilding is present it is metallic looking.

Where broken, the break edges will have the appearance of glass and the edges will be sharp. The interior will be solid throughout. Sherds may have edges sharp enough to cut fingers.

Cracks will usually be fine and straight. No crazing or crackling is found on hard paste glaze, but occasionally occurs on some old soft paste porcelains.

Hard paste rings with a metallic sound similar to glass when struck on the edge. If a dull sound is produced, could have been repaired or is pottery.

On hard paste pottery look and feel for spiral ridges on the inside of bowls and vases. This indicates wreathing, a strengthening technique that was used only on hard paste ware.

Bone china

Bone china was developed and used mainly in Britain from the 1750s but was perfected around 1794 by Josiah Spode (most of the world's bone china is still made in Britain). Bone china quickly became popular, for duties on imported Chinese wares were becoming extremely high. By 1918 all the major potteries were making it.

Strictly speaking, bone china is soft paste porcelain but it has the translucency and hardness of hard paste. Calcined bone ash (usually ox bone roasted or partially fused in the kiln then ground to a powder) was added to hard paste ingredients (50 per cent animal bone, 25 per cent china clay, 25 per cent china stone). This recipe reduced distortion during firing, so was more economical and provided a durable service at a far lower cost than soft paste porcelain, which it quickly replaced. The term bone china was not used until 1836. The bone ash makes the ceramic body an ivory white in colour.

Though not as hard as true porcelain, bone china is harder and more durable than soft-paste porcelain. It does not have the cold, glassy look and feel of hard paste.
The bone ash greatly increases the translucence of the porcelain and it can be tested in the same way as porcelain. Hold a hand or finger behind the item and the shadow should be seen through the fabric.

Enamel colours and gold are brighter than on other porcelains. The glaze will not chip, crack or scratch.

Maker's marks that include the words 'bone china' are twentieth century. If the mark has a country's name but not 'made in' then it is from 1890 to the first quarter of the twentieth century.

Dating pottery backstamps

Pottery maker's marks are innumerable, and, as many publications exist with comprehensive listings, they are therefore not covered here. Only a few general guidelines are given.

Registration marks

Registration marks were used by pottery (also retailers, wholesalers, manufacturers) companies to register their designs or shapes with the British Patent Office in London, and were valid for a period of three years. However, the date applies only to when the copyright was allocated; the design or item itself could have been made years later. The same diamond registration design was used for a variety of products. Class IV refers to pottery; Class III for instance, refers to glass objects. Two diamond designs were used but they date to different periods.

If the design is difficult to make out, hold up the plate to the light.

1842–1867
Year Letter

A: 1845	J: 1854	S: 1849
B: 1858	K: 1857	T: 1867
C: 1844	L: 1856	U: 1848
D: 1852	M: 1859	V: 1850
E: 1855	N: 1864	W: 1865
F: 1847	O: 1862	X: 1842
G: 1863	P: 1851	Y: 1853
H: 1843	Q: 1866	Z: 1860
I: 1846	R: 1861	

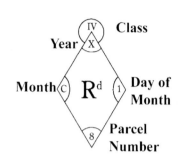

1868–1883
Year Letter

A: 1871	K: 1883
C: 1870	P: 1877
D: 1878	S: 1875
E: 1881	U: 1874
F: 1873	V: 1876
H: 1869	W: 1878
I: 1872	X: 1868
J: 1880	Y: 1879
L: 1882	

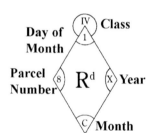

Month Letters
These apply to both designs:

A	December	H	April
B	October	I	July
C or O	January	K	November & December 1860
D	September	M	June
E	May	R	August & 1 to 19 September 1857
G	February	W	March

Registered numbers

These replaced the diamond design and the numbers are preceded by 'Rd 12345' or 'Rd No. 12345'

1884: 1	1912: 594195	1940: 837520
1885: 19756	1913: 612431	1941: 838590
1886: 40480	1914: 630190	1942: 839230
1887: 64520	1915: 644935	1943: 839980
1888: 90483	1916: 653521	1944: 841040
1889: 116648	1917: 658988	1945: 842670
1890: 141273	1918: 662872	1946: 845550
1891: 163767	1919: 666128	1947: 849790
1892: 185713	1920: 673750	1948: 853260
1893: 205240	1921: 680147	1949: 856999
1894: 224720	1922: 687144	1950: 860854
1895: 246975	1923: 694999	1951: 863970
1896: 268392	1924: 702671	1952: 866280
1897: 291241	1925: 710165	1953: 869300
1898: 311658	1926: 718057	1954: 872531
1899: 331707	1927: 726330	1955: 876067
1900: 351202	1928: 734370	1956: 879282
1901: 368154	1929: 742725	1957: 882949
1902: 385180	1930: 751160	1958: 887079
1903: 403200	1931: 760583	1959: 891665
1904: 424400	1932: 769670	1960: 895000
1905: 447800	1933: 779292	1961: 899914
1906: 471860	1934: 789019	1962: 904638
1907: 493900	1935: 799097	1963: 909364
1908: 518640	1936: 808794	1964: 914536
1909: 535170	1937: 817293	1965: 919607
1910: 552000	1938: 825231	
1911: 574817	1939: 832610	

Royal: in trademarks after 1850

Limited or **Ltd**: After the 1860 Companies Act; not usually on pottery until after 1880

Trade Mark: after 1862 when Trade Mark Act passed; not normally on pottery until 1875

England: the American McKinley Tariff Act of 1891 decreed that imports had to show the country of origin. The word England therefore does not appear prior to 1891

Bone china: twentieth century

Made in England: after 1914, generally twentieth century

Name of a pattern: after 1810

Chapter 4
DOMESTIC MATERIALS

Roman building material

Tiles

On any Roman site a quantity of roofing material is likely to be recovered. Most of the finds will be imbrix and tegulae (see below). A normal roof covered with these will result in a collection of approximately 2:1 tegula to imbrix.

If there is any confusion about whether the find is pottery or building material, look at the back. A rough surface may show the evidence of sand, grass/straw or other surface upon which the tiles were left to dry. Pottery will usually show the lines of either a coil-built or a wheel-thrown piece (see page 113).

Tegula

A wide roof tile, either square or rectangular in shape, with flanges on its longitudinal sides. Sometimes has a nail hole near one edge. A tegula is usually 430mm x 250–280mm but can be larger. Tapered in width, it is narrower at the bottom, shaped to fit into the one below.

Imbrix

A narrow, semi-cylindrical tile, slightly tapering at one end to fit into the wider opening of the one joining it. It would have been placed face downwards to cover the joint between two tegula, then mortared to the tegula to form a waterproof seal.

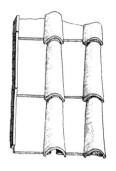

Roman tiles are usually an orange/red colour with a grey interior. Cream examples are fairly common and it is these which are most regularly confused with amphorae.

Occasionally there may be animal footprints of dogs, chickens, cats, etc. Other marks may be human footprints, or rain drops.

A number of tiles will include semi-circular lines. These are the marks of individual makers and, often consist of three fingers that have been dragged around in a circle. Other tiles may have more or fewer, rings. One hypothesis is that the three may represent 30 tiles made.

A dog print: It is the claw marks above the paw that define a dog print, cats withdraw their claws when walking so cannot be seen on print marks.

Antefix:

A small, often triangular piece to close off the roof at the edges. These are often plain but decorated examples can be found (right).

They have a domed foot at the rear to slot into the curve of the imbrix.

One of the most famous examples is the one illustrated here of the XX Legion found at Holt, Clwyd, Wales (size 12cm).

Stamps often appear on all Roman ceramic building material but particularly on tegulae and bricks (about 1 in 10). If there is a stamp on an imbrix it is usually on the side, rarely on the top. They are usually rectangular or round and impressed from a wooden block. They appear on both civilian and military building materials.

Bricks

There are essentially seven types of Roman brick:

1. 19cm length x 18.5cm width x 2.5cm thickness;
2. 2.22cm x 22cm x 3.5cm (*laterculus bessialis*);
3. 30cm x 30.5cm x 3.0cm (*later tetradoros*);
4. 40cm x 40cm x 4.0cm (*sesquipedalis*);
5. 40.5cm x 29.5cm x 3.5cm (*lydion*);
6. 55cm x 55cm x 4.5cm (*bipedale*); and
7. 28cm+ x 19cm x 3.5cm

Roman bricks are broad and thin and more like tiles. They come in many shapes and sizes, including circular, and were used for many different purposes. No. 5 is the most common and is used primarily for walling. No. 2 is often used for hypocaust pillars.

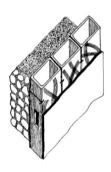

Roman flue tiles

Flue tiles were used in heating systems, either behind a wall or under a hypocaust.

The vent opening at the centre of the narrower sides is about 9cm x 4cm but sometimes they are circular.

They vary in type but the most common is an about 41 cm long, 15cm wide and 10cm deep.

Both ends are open and both wide sides are keyed (narrow sides plain) in order to provide a bed for the mortar.

The tiles were made by wrapping clay around a wooden form, cutting holes, then scored with a comb or die rolled over surface, to provide a keyed surface. Scored or incised surfaces can range from various geometrical patterns to ornate pictures or even graffiti. They can be made using fingers, combs or roller-dies although roller-dies are not common and were used predominantly in the south-east from c.AD 75–175 during three phases, AD 75–90, AD 120–125, and AD 155–175. Impressed patterned flue tiles date from AD 80 to AD 150 although they were reused up to AD 200.

Tiles can also carry stamps of the army, government of the province and some towns.

Medieval roof tiles

Ceramic earthenware roof tiles appeared predominantly in South-East England from the mid-twelfth century and were copied in form from oak shingles. They became widespread in popularity by the thirteenth century. They were made locally so appear in a number of fabrics but generally most are some shade of red.

Flanged

The earliest of the medieval roof tiles, they were made in a mould with the flanges being finished by hand. In appearance they seem similar to Roman tegulae but are smaller in size with smaller flanges. They also have nail holes and are glazed down the middle of tile unlike their Roman equivalent. Like their Roman counterparts they will often show evidence of tally marks.

In early tiles there is generally a uniform glaze on the upper surface, but in later tiles the glaze is only splashed on, sometimes only on the exposed lower third of the tile.

Approximate sizes:
Length: 350mm
Breadth: 250-300mm
Thickness: 30mm
Weight: 3.3kg

Hole for securing with an oak peg or a nail

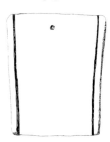

Tapered to cater for overlap

Curved

Curved tiles are similar to Roman imbrix but, like the flange tiles are smaller and have a nail hole. They come in various sizes but are approximately:

Length: 340mm x 140mm (narrow end)-180 (broad end) mm
Breadth: 140–190mm
Thickness: 8–25mm
Weight: 1.6kg

Nail hole at narrow end

Tapered to allow overlap

Some tiles may show finger marks of the maker gripping the tile whilst it is still wet. There may also be marks from where the tiles were laid to dry, including grass or straw marks on the reverse of the tiles, paw prints or, more rarely, rain drop depressions.

All were made in sanded moulds, so look for quartz flecks on the reverse side where sand has adhered to the wet clay.

Shoulder peg

The name comes from the shape of the tile, which tapers halfway down each side, forming a cricket bat shape. The shoulder peg tile is generally thicker than the plain peg tile and has rounded edges.

Approximate sizes:
Length: 310mm
Breadth: 200-140mm
Thickness: 16-22mm
Weight: 2kg

The heavier weight of the shoulder tile meant a much heavier roof than one made of the flanged and curved, or the peg tiles.

The peg tile usually had a single hole, which was square, circular or diamond-shaped.

The shoulder tile would overlap some two thirds of the length of the lower tile.

Plain peg

The plain peg tile appeared in the late twelfth to early thirteenth centuries and is the most commonly found tile of
the thirteenth century. This is probably because they were
cheap and quick to make as they needed no further work
once removed from the mould.

Plain 'peg' tiles were being made at Clarendon Palace in
the late twelfth century, and the kiln used to make them is
on display at the British Museum.

They have one or two round or square holes punched
through the fabric, although not all go right through. They
would have been secured to the laths on the roof with iron
nails or, more rarely, wooden pegs. Another method was
for the lath to have projecting nibs of clay to fit the nail
holes.

Glaze, if present, covers the bottom third of the surface.

There are a number of different fabrics and a variety of
sizes, but these tiles are usually rectangular.

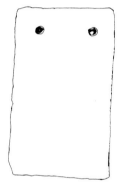

Approximate sizes:
Length; 260mm
Breadth; 170mm
Thickness; 9-18mm
Weight; 1.3kg

Peg tiles would overlap about half of the tile beneath.

As previously stated, most tiles varied enormously. A
Statute of 1477 gave a standard dimension of 265mm x
160mm x 16mm. However, it was not adhered to and tiles
would still vary in size from place to place. Today the
British Standard (of 1959) is 266mm x 165mm x 38mm.

Medieval floor tiles

Placing ceramic earthenware tiles on the floor as a decorative covering and to provide a hard-wearing surface in both ecclesiastical and civil buildings began in the mid-thirteenth century but did not become widespread until the fourteenth. Early tile production was dominated by the church and some of the earliest tiles in the country can be seen at Salisbury Cathedral (begun 1223). However after the Black Death (1348) tile production became more commercial. Most of the medieval tiles are warm in colour as a result of adding metals to a lead glaze. If iron was added the result would be a dark brown, while copper would give green, and in large amounts, black.

Many original medieval floors can still be seen, particularly in religious buildings.

There are many varieties of medieval tile but four examples are noted here: the plain mosaic tile, two decorative tiles (the Westminster and Penn) and the plain tile.

Plain mosaic tiles like tesserae were made in a variety of geometric shapes. The earliest known are at Fountains Abbey, Yorkshire (1211–1247) and Canterbury Cathedral, c.1220. They are used often in Cistercian abbeys.

They are mall tiles 50mm square.

In the fourteenth century a two-coloured pattern of alternated dark green and yellow tiles was popular.

The two decorative tiles are of the type known as *encaustic*, which means that they are stamped to leave an impression and then filled with a contrasting coloured liquid clay body. When the tile was dry the excess clay (overfill) was scraped away to reveal the design. The tile was then covered with a lead glaze and fired.

The clays used were generally the same as for roof tiles but a variety of body clays, slips, inlays and glazes were used to produce different colours.

The designs were usually impressed with wooden relief stamps but these could be reused to the point where they wore out and produced blurred images. This was also true of designs which were copied and recopied until they bore little resemblance to the original. Many tiles show mistakes where the carver of the wooden block forgot to reverse the design.

Often a selection of tiles would be laid together and then bordered by tiles of a plain, contrasting colour. This not only saved on making the more expensive tiles, but also highlighted the designs.

Westminster tiles are so called as they were first recognised in the Muniment Room at Westminster Abbey. They date to the mid thirteenth–fourteenth century and have three distinct size groups:

101–2mm in length/breadth x 25–7mm thickness
110–120mm x 25–30mm
126–37mm x 22–7mm

Decorative tiles were made either by *inlaying* or *printing* the design. With the inlaying system a design was pressed into the clay with a stamp and yellow pipeclay spread into the hollows. Printing involved the pipeclay being spread directly onto the raised area of a stamp which was then pressed directly into the clay. The difference can be difficult to identify but generally with inlaid tiles the pipeclay is thick and the edges of the design are clear. With printed tiles the design lines are not so clear cut and if the pipeclay has been spread too liberally on the stamp it can result in a smudged design as the clay swells out. Printing was cheaper and quicker. Sgraffito designs were engraved through a coat of clay to allow the brown background to show through.

Penn tiles are named after their place of manufacture at Penn, Buckinghamshire, and date to *c.*1350–1390.

They were used in many churches as they were cheap and mass produced. There are three sizes. The largest is the earliest and they are generally the best fired and have the most interesting designs. These were followed by a slightly smaller size, less well made, with a lot of repeated patterns.

105–15mm length/breadth x 19–26mm thickness
119–31mm x 22–7mm
131–6mm x 22–6mm

Designs vary from tile to tile and can be floral, heraldic, or show mythic beasts, but probably the most common is the *fleur de lys*. Often a design was complete in itself on one tile, while on others the design would be covered by many tiles, such as Chapter House in Westminster Abbey (1255).

On the reverse of tiles there are often scoop marks made before the tile was fired. They are intended to provide a greater adhesion.

Scoop marks

During the fourteenth–sixteenth centuries plain glazed Flemish floor tiles were imported, although some may have been made locally. The Flemish tiles were generally fired, glazed and fired again whereas the English tiles were generally glazed and fired, but this is difficult to detect by eye. Some have no glaze at all. They are plain, glazed tiles in a predominantly dark green-brown or yellow glaze over a white slip. Floors would be laid out in a chequerboard pattern of alternating colours. Flemish tiles often have holes in the corner of the upper surface.

Flemish tiles

Bricks

Up to the end of the twelfth century, Roman bricks and tiles were often reused and few bricks were being made. Brickmaking began again in earnest in the thirteenth century, since when brick has become the most common building material in Britain, being cheaper and lighter than stone. The size has varied little over the centuries so bricks can be difficult to date. The following guidelines are approximate, as handmade bricks are subject to fluctuations such as shrinkage, but generally bricks have always been about the size of a man's hand.

Some bricks have tally marks whilst others have marks common to all handmade ceramic building material that is left to air dry. Grass or straw marks, on which materials they were usually laid, rain drop impressions, paw prints and finger marks particularly where edges have been smoothed down are also often visible.

Twelfth-century bricks were large and thin, approximately 280mm–330mm x 125–150mm x 45–70mm, and are generally called 'Great Bricks'. They were found in various buildings in East Anglia up to the early sixteenth century.

Mid-thirteenth-century Flemish bricks were imported in great quantity and are approximately 200–250mm x 95–120mm x 45–65mm, smaller than local ones. They are called 'Statute Bricks' to distinguish them from the Great Brick.

In the mid-fifteenth century there was a great increase in the domestic use of bricks and the common size was now 240mm x 115mm x 50mm. However, they were still very irregular in size and shape and needed thick mortar joints of about 15–25mm to even out the discrepancies. Small quantities of Dutch bricks were imported with a size of 152–209mm x 76–95mm x 36–44mm.

Medieval bricks were usually made in a sanded mould so look for a rough under-surface.

In 1769 brick size was standardised by law at 209mm x 101mm x 63mm. In 1784 these bricks were taxed in order to meet expenses for the American Wars. As they were taxed by quantity, not size, it was economically viable to make the bricks bigger, so the size increased to 234mm x 114mm x 114mm.

Bricks were now greatly improved with better blending of clays and better firing and moulding techniques, which resulted in more uniformity in shape and size. Colours changed according to fashion with red, purple or grey being the most common until *c.*1730, when brownish or pinkish grey became popular.

By the 1700s a shallow depression was included in the brick to provide keying for the mortar.

Realising manufacturers were getting away with paying less tax on the larger bricks, the government responded in 1803 by charging double duty on bricks exceeding 150 cubic inches (2,458cc) so the size changed again, this time to 228mm x 114mm x 76mm. In 1850 the duty was repealed.

After 1858 most bricks were made by machinery, which produced even more uniformity and reduced the cost, therefore making them accessible to everyone. Brickwork now abounds, with more bricks being made than ever before.

By the mid-eighteenth century, grey was in vogue, but this was followed by yellow around 1800 as it was believed that this was a closer imitation of classical buildings. By the nineteenth century, the shallow depression seen previously became the deep frogging still seen on today's bricks. With the greater uniformity of machine made bricks, mortar joints were reduced to 8mm.

The current British Standard 3921 of 1985 for a brick is 215mm x 102.5mm x 65mm – practically identical to the Flemish brick of 700 years ago. 1965 legislation required thermal insulation so bricks were replaced by concrete blocks. Mechanisation has allowed the production of a variety of bricks such as the perforated type.

Bricks also come in variety of shapes and sizes that serve specific applications, such as the dog-leg brick for angles.

Glass wine bottles

There is little evidence of wine bottles before 1592 but by 1634 English manufacture was well established. Even so, they still had to compete with bellarmines (see page 123) and Delftware (see page 125) wine pots.

From the mid-seventeenth century a duty was imposed on the importation and manufacture of clear glass, so bottles were always coloured until 1845 when the tax was repealed.

Dating can only be taken as a broad outline, because wine bottles were handmade and many variations occur, with certain designs continuing in use after others had appeared. Some more remote glass houses may have been behind the times, so designs often overlap. Features come and go: for instance the neck, which starts out parallel in form, becomes squatter, and then returns to parallel. Bottles recovered in a partial state they can be difficult to date accurately.

Pontil mark

As the bottle was being worked it was held by an iron rod (iron does not conduct heat) attached to the base of the bottle and opposite the blowpipe. When the bottle was ready the rod was snapped away leaving a round jagged reminder of where it was attached (see right). This is true of all glass work until the mid-1800's when the use of moulds did away with the pontil.

A pontil mark looks like a ring.

Shaft and globe

Dimensions of shaft and globe 1660-1900
From 10.5 x 9.5 to 23 x 13cm

1630–50

String-rim is low, up to 12-15mm. It has rounded edges, noticeably protruding from the neck.

A globular body with a narrow neck meant the sediments remained in the body and were less likely to end in the drinker's glass. Until the early nineteenth-century bottles were blown so the surface is free of seam lines.

The kick-up is shallow so the bottle does not sit comfortably. The Pontil mark is low, almost to the same length as the bottle walls and could scratch the table.

The colour is generally pale green with a few dark green.

1660–80

Most shaft and globe bottles come from this period.

The string-rim is nearer the top and the neck is shorter and no longer parallel, as it tapers at the shoulders.

It has an egg-shaped body with a deeper and wider kick-up. The bottle does not sit comfortably.

Most are now dark green.

Onion, c. 1680-1730

The string-rim is now around 6mm from top. By 1700 it is 3–4mm from top and instead of being round is now more V-shaped.

The neck is much shorter and sunk into the shoulders and accounts for half the height of the bottle.

The body is larger and more squat; the weight has increased and the bottle sits more comfortably with a wider and shallower kick-up.

The colour is mainly green but other colours were being introduced.

A 1636 Act forbade the selling of wine by the bottle as, being handmade, they were subject to enormous variation. So the client would go to the vintner and the wine was decanted straight from the cask into bottles. This brought about the practice around 1660 of adding personal seals to the bottles. The most popular period for seals is 1680–1730.

Seals were normally circular and ranged in size from 6.45cm to 4.44cm in diameter. During the period 1670–85 a cushion of glass was added to the bottle body and a seal attached to it. These seals have often been found on their own. Thereafter seals were applied directly to a pad of molten glass. If the glass was too molten the seal appears blurred, if too hard then the seal is indistinct.

Seals were generally divided into two; those for innkeepers which usually showed the sign of the inn, and those for private ownership. Later private seals included stock bought pseudo-heraldic arms.

Dimensions of onion:
Small onion, c.1680–1720:
Height; 14-18cm
Width; 13-15cm

Medium onion, c.1710–20:
Height; 18-19cm
Width; 13cm-15cm

Large onion, c.1710–20:
Height; 19-22cm
Width; 13-15cm

Many onion bottles are imports particularly from the Netherlands, Germany and France. Dutch onions are lighter in weight and colour than English. The string rims are flatter and the kick-up is lower. Continental bottles do not have seals.

Mallet, c.1725–60

In the eighteenth century, port became popular. Port needs to mature in the bottle and this led to a change in bottle design. Straight sides were required as the bottle needed to be laid down horizontally so the contents would keep in contact with the cork. If the cork was not kept moist it would dry and shrivel thereby allowing the contents to leak out.

Mallet bottles first appeared *c*.1725 and became common *c*.1730–40 but were on the wane by around 1750. They are similar to the onion.

The neck length approximately equalled or slightly exceeded the body length. However, by *c*.1730 very long necks appear and these exceed the body dimensions.

A wider range of colours was now available, including pale green, amber, dark green.

The body squarer and more shouldered and the kick-up is in its most exaggerated form and reaches to mid-body length.

The base is very broad and exceeds the body length.

©TT

Cylindrical, c.1740–1830

The true cylindrical bottle first appeared *c*.1735, and bodies vary from cylindrical to squat cylindrical, which appeared *c*.1740. By 1780–90 the true cylindrical form was the most common, but squat was still popular until 1790–1800. The cylindrical bottle lasted for over a century so was very popular.

Squat cylinder

At the beginning of the period, the string-rim projected below the top but later forms are more band-like in appearance.

By 1770 there were two rims, called 'double string-rim'.

Necks are short and stumpy. There were few long necks after 1765.

The body height exceeds base and the kick-up is wider and deeper but rarely as deep as mallets. Very few were of light coloured glass.

The base to shoulder measurement is approximately one and one-third times the base diameter.

True Cylinder

String rims now have a neat cone shape which change little from now on.

The bottle gets progressively taller, narrower in the body, and shorter in neck. There are few long necks after 1760.

By *1770* the angular shoulders give way to more rounded shoulders with a medium body.

The kick-up is neater, shallower, and more cone-shaped; the base to shoulder height is at least one and a half times the base diameter.

Oval seals are a feature of the nineteenth century and are often found on wine or beer merchants' bottles. By then seals were more of an advertisement and less personalised.

Three-piece mould cylindrical bottle, c. 1811-1900

The string-rim is nearly cone-shaped, and two-tier, which alters little over the next 30 years. It was still separately applied and not moulded integrally until 1900.

Mould lines clearly seen but by 1890-1900 mould marks begin to become less apparent.

Base concave and shallow with embossed lettering. Fewer bottles sealed.

Embossing continued on many glass bottles until the early twentieth century when paper labelling replaced much of the embossing. Certain manufacturers retained the practice.

The three-piece mould bottle was developed in *c.*1821 and within ten years most production was made in this way. This resulted in more bottles being produced and of better quality.

By 1840 the new moulds did away with the pontil its distinctive mark disappears.

In 1903 a fully automatic blowing machine was perfected, thereby making mechanical glassblowing possible.

(Drawings adapted from Dumbrell)

Cleaning bottles

Clean with cool water and a soft cloth.

Do not use hot water as this may crack the glass.

Do not use an abrasive cleaner as this may cause scratches.

Do not force anything too large down the neck as it may crack.

Extremely soiled glass bottles can be cleaned by soaking overnight in a mixture of a water softener such as Calgon and water. To clean the interior, fill the the bottle to at least half way and add a handful of uncooked rice or clean sand. Gently swirl to dislodge any dirt. Do not wash the rice or sand down the sink or drain as it will block the pipe.

Drinking glasses

Drinking glasses were rare before the reign of Charles II. Silver, pottery, leather, horn and wooden vessels were used beforehand.

Prior to *c*.1675 most fine glass was imported, particularly from Venice. However, this early glass had impurities in the glass (or 'metal' as it is called in the industry), and as it had a cloudy appearance, it was considered unsuitable for quality production. It was not until George Ravenscroft mixed a lead oxide and potash into the metal that a high quality fine glass was produced. The lead made the glass heavy, strong, highly refractive and elastic so it could be stretched into the popular long stems, engraved and faceted into different shapes. Lead glass was immediately admired for its beauty and clarity and so became extremely popular. Drinking glasses were then made in their thousands in the eighteenth century, making England the leading glass producer of the world. Also, its highly refractive ability made it invaluable for the optic industry and played a part in the development of telescopes and microscopes.

Feet

There are many different types of foot. However, three types predominate:

Folded foot

From *c*.1680–1746 drinking glasses had a foot which included a fold under its rim approximately 4–5mm thick, which prevented chipping. When the 1745–6 excise tax levied a charge on glass by weight the folded foot was phased out in order to lighten the vessel.

The underside of the foot is concave to prevent the pontil mark scratching the surface of the table.

Domed foot

The domed foot is usually associated with the folded foot. It gave way to the large plain foot with a high arched instep, which gradually diminished until small and flat.

The use of the pontil mark was phased out c.1825 with new moulding techniques and the high conical foot also disappeared.

Conical foot

The folded and domed feett were replaced by a sharp edge that chipped easily, so rounded feet replaced these and remained thereafter.

The foot became flatter and shallower as no gap was needed to account for a pontil mark.

The diameter of the foot should be wider than that of the bowl.

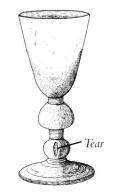

Stems

Stems are generally the best means of dating a drinking glass.

Heavy balusters

The earliest stems, c.1680–1735, are the heavy baluster in two styles: inverted and the true baluster (named after the architectural feature).

They consist of a swollen bulge in the stem called a knop. A stem could have one or more knops and often a bubble or tear within them. Towards the end of the period the knops were less heavy and are replaced by a variety of shapes, such as acorns, cylinders, and rarer egg-shapes.

Tear

Base of bowl very thick

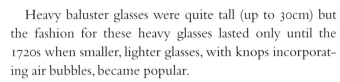

Heavy baluster glasses were quite tall (up to 30cm) but the fashion for these heavy glasses lasted only until the 1720s when smaller, lighter glasses, with knops incorporating air bubbles, became popular.

Light balusters, c.1720–1750

As their name suggests, they are lighter in weight than the heavy balusters. They also have longer stems with more complex and wider spaced knops. The base of the bowl is thinner and the whole has a more elegant appearance. The tear in the stem disappears after the introduction of the air twist.

Plain stems, c. 1700–1775

The bowl tends to be trumpet and the stem is tapered towards the foot often with a tear. The foot is conical and in early versions is folded, but this disappears around 1745.

Plain stem 1700-40

- With tears 1700-40
- Without tears 1720-1800
- Incised 1700–40

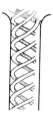

Air twist stems were also developed in an attempt to lighten the vessel and to avoid the 1745–6 excise tax. They date from around 1730 to *c.*1775 and have many forms with as many as 12 filaments in a spiral. The earliest is the twist simply filled with air. By around 1750 an opaque white was added to make the air twist more visible. By *c.*1760 colour (usually green or red) had been added to twists and by the mid-1770 the multi-spiral air twist stems were extremely popular.

Colour air twist stems have a visible join at both ends of the stem

The whole glass still feels quite heavy. Early eighteenth-century air twist glasses usually have a trumpet bowl and the air twist extends into the bowl (upper left). The bowl, which has a grey tone, is usually free of decoration. The foot is folded, with a pontil mark.

Main air-twist, 1730–60
- Plain air twist with drawn bowl, 1730-45
- Knopped air spirals with applied bowls, 1740-60
- Silver or mercury spirals, 1740-60

Main white opaque air-twist, 1750-80
- Single and compound opaque spirals, 1750-80
- Mixed with mercury spiral, 1760-80
- Mixed with one or more coloured spiral, 1760-80

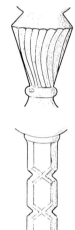

Pedestal or *Silesian* glasses, *c.*1715–65, have a conical bowl, broad shoulders tapering towards a conical foot, and a moulded stem divided by ribs into four, six or eight sides. The glass tends to be heavy with a grey tone, and if engraving is present it is usually of a Dutch subject.

*Faceted glasses, c.*1760–1810, have stems that are divided into hexagonal sections with facets of diamond, hexagonal or straight. Overall the glasses are well balanced and elegant. The have a flat foot with no fold, but wide and fluted with the pontil marks ground out. Engraved decoration on the bowls tends to be of vines, stars, flowers, birds and insects.

Bowls

Dating by bowl can only be limited as most types have a long life.

Lead glass differs from soda glass in tht it is heavier in weight, and more resonant. It chimes when tapped lightly on the rim with a fingernail. Soda glass by comparison gives a dull thud. Leaded glass also is distinguishable by a faint grayish/blue tinge with 'oily' feel.

The earliest bowls were mainly funnel shaped and are heavy with indentations and striations. Striations appear on all handmade glasses and are caused by the tool forming the bowl whilst being rotated. They can be seen better on thin glass.

Bell-shaped and waisted, beginning of the eighteenth century

Trumpet: beginning of eighteenth century

Early glass was also very brittle. This was improved around 1740, after the introduction of the Perrot furnace in 1734, which produced a higher and more uniform temperature than was previously possible. This resulted in a more uniform glass without the dark tinge of earlier pieces.

Ogee: c.1720–5 onwards

Bucket: c.1775 onwards

Waisted bucket: c.1775–6 onwards

Rounded funnel: beginning of the eighteenth century onwards

Ovoid: similar to today; beginning of eighteenth century onwards

Engraving

Engraving was introduced on glass in around 1735 (although older glasses were often engraved at a later date). There is a wide variety of subjects but wine glasses were usually engraved with vines or grapes; ale glasses often had barley and hops; cider glasses had apples, apple trees and the word 'Cyder'. Flowers and plants were popular as well as animals, ships, etc.

Care

Sudden temperature changes will crack any glass, particularly old glass; therefore wash in tepid water.

Take care if washing glass with gloves on as they can be very slippery. Use a plastic bowl so that if the item is dropped it will not break. This will also reduce the chance of accidental damage against a hard edge like that of a sink.

Use cleaning cloths carefully; they can snag on broken edges.

If there is a cloudiness or milkiness about the surface this can indicate that the glass has deteriorated and therefore should not be cleaned. Seek conservation advice.

Tapping *very* gently against the rim with a fingernail should give a clear sound; if instead there is a dull sound this may indicate a break or a repair which may not be obvious to the eye. If a breakage is suspected ensure it is packaged carefully.

Let items air-dry.

Knives
Fourteenth-century examples

During the fourteenth century, the length of the blade of a knife was roughly equal to the haft. The blade would have been longer only if made for a special purpose.

Where the handle met the blade there was often a copper-alloy band, or bolster, to protect the handle. At the end of the blade would be a notch (a *choil*), which would prevent the bolster being scratched when the blade was sharpened. This was a feature of blades from the Bronze Age until the eighteenth century.

There may have been ring finials, to enable the knife to be hung on a belt. this method was often used by those who could not afford a leather sheath for the knife.

In 1365 a decree of Edward III required maker's marks to be included on the blade. There are a great number of marks and they could often change hands, so do not rely on them.

Marks were generally inlaid into the blade in copper or brass, on the left side (viewed with tip pointing away from holder), at the back of the blade and close to the handle as this is the thickest part of the blade.

The blade terminates in a long, thin spike (tang) onto which the handle is attached. There are a variety of methods of attachment. The simplest is the whittle tang and occurs in two forms; a pointed, or pin, tang onto which a cylindrical handle, such as antler, was simply hammered.

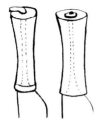

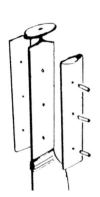

The knock-on tang was most common but the through tang was more secure.

The through tang ran the length of the handle and protruded beyond. The protruding end was then either curled back on itself (sometimes called a candle end as it resembled a wick), or a metal plate or cap was attached to obscure the tang end.

The handles come in a variety of materials: copper, brass, tin, horn, bone, antler, wood and occasionally leather. Ivory was for the affluent.

By the end of fourteenth century, a fundamental change occurred. Instead of solid handles fixed onto a whittle tang, many knives had composite handles.

At this point, the tang becomes a flat 'scale' pierced with holes. Two separate scales of antler, bone, etc were placed each side and through rivets added. Often an end cap would be added. The handles are usually wider than those on whittle tangs.

Fifteenth-century examples

Throughout medieval times a steel strip was often added on to a knife's edge. Steel was being imported from Sweden, Russia and Spain and was expensive, so was used sparingly to create a sharp and more durable cutting edge. Striations on a blade may indicate the knife once had a steel edge.

The previous bolster consisting of a strip of copper-alloy was replaced by an integrally forged bolster around 1509.

Blades became longer, sharp-pointed, narrower and more elegant.

Scale-tanged knives did not have bolsters, so a pair of tin shoulders were soldered or riveted on to separate the blade from the haft.

Finials were often decorated with alloy caps. More decorative examples have copper alloy horse's hooves, animal heads, or hammered or engraved lines.

Sixteenth-century examples

The introduction of forks coincided with knife points becoming blunter, as they were no longer needed to spear food.

By the mid-sixteenth century the norm was for the whole blade to be made of the stronger steel.

The bolster and the tang were now one unit and forged onto the steel blade.

Knives in this period were often made in pairs; one to keep dry for cutting bread and one to cut meat and lift food to the mouth. However, most were still used mainly for serving food rather than eating with.

Knives were now more balanced, thin and very elegant. Fine-quality knives known as 'Sunday knives' were popular and were often worn at religious festivals. Black ebony hafts were often used at Lent, white ivory or mother-of-pearl for Easter and a combination of two for Pentecost. Hafts sometimes had detachable toothpicks.

Seventeenth-century examples

During the Commonwealth, points went out of fashion. The 'Puritan' knife was very plain and itself fell from favour with the Restoration (1660).

In 1606 the Cutler's Company of London introduced a quality control mark of an upright dagger, which appeared alongside the maker's trademark.

The cutlers were responsible only for the blades. The handles were made by separately by other specialists.

During the seventeenth century, the habit of using knife and fork together began to emerge. Knives, forks and spoons were still personal possessions and had to be carried when dining out, as these were not supplied.

Not until the turn of the century (c. 1695–1720) and the 'dognose' pattern were sets of flatware (non-ferrous forks and spoons as opposed to cutlery, ferrous bladed knives and forks) laid together.

Cutler's dagger mark

Eighteenth-century examples

At the end of the seventeenth century, the blade swept into a curved scimitar, a style which continued throughout much of the eighteenth century. There are three main scimitar types, the second two having a distinctive hump on the back of the blade.

The blunt blades are wide and round and would have doubled as a spoon, picking up food that was beyond the capabilities of the two-tined fork.

1690-1730   1720–50

The handles were pistol-shaped, a shape particular to the British, and could be very decorative. From *c.*1720, ceramic handles were introduced, usually blue and white to match the range of Chinese-influenced items at this time. Many, due to their fragility, have not survived. Ivory stained green was popular throughout the eighteenth century, and was nearly always mounted with a silver cap. Silver handles are usually a mere thin covering with the handle filled with resin, shellac or pitch (for care of these see page 10). These 'silver' handles do not include hallmarks or maker's marks as the silver was so thin it was below the minimum required to be hallmarked. The silver handles are often thin and badly worn. The scimitar knife disappeared around the 1770s.

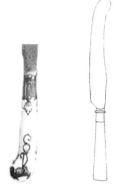

1740–60

By the middle of the eighteenth century, there was a change in fashion from the scimitar to a French-style blade, following the general rise in neoclassicism.

The scimitar blade was replaced by a more spear-pointed, straight blade.

The bolster almost forms a right angle doing away with the choil.

The pistol handles was replaced by a flat-ended or diagonally truncated haft, often from green-stained ivory. Hafts were dominated by ivory, and silver. Bone, horn and wood continued to be used for more utilitarian purposes. Also popular was mother-of-pearl, as it did not split in dry weather.

Nineteenth and twentieth-century examples

In 1840 in Birmingham, a method of silver-plating was invented which involved placing a thin layer of silver over a base metal, usually nickel silver an alloy of copper, zinc and nickel. This method was used especially on more expensive knives with a base of carbon steel, as the steel tainted the food. This new process made knife production very cheap. By the end of the nineteenth century, knives were being mass-produced in steel.

Stainless steel was developed in 1914 in Sheffield, and thereafter, British knife blades were usually made in Sheffield. Stainless steel is extremely strong, rust resistant, easy to maintain and will not taint the taste of food. For this reason it was now possible to make fish and salad knives from steel as previously only silver could be used with these foods. It was also now possible to produce a one-piece knife.

From c.1865, a host of plastics were introduced, initially in an attempt to imitate ivory (see page 49). When celluloid was invented it quickly became the dominant plastic and replaced not only ivory, but horn, amber and tortoiseshell. Sheffield cutlers are estimated to have made some 20 million celluloid knife-handles each year. Celluloid ivory is often made with the long growth lines typical of elephant ivory, but it does not have the cross-hatching. It was commonly manufactured until the 1930s.

The typical twentieth-century knife had a parallel-sided steel blade

Care of knives, forks and spoons

Many of these are composite items and so care must be taken when cleaning each part. Conserve according to the material at most risk.

Try to keep the use of water to a minimum.

Many knives and forks have a resin within the handle to secure it to the blade. If immersed in hot water the resin softens and the blade may become detached. Alternatively the water may cause the join to swell and split. The difficulty with the resin used in knife construction is that over the years manufacturers tried a great variety of glues and some are more unstable than others.

Some blades may appear to be very black and often much worn; these are usually carbon steel knives, which have suffered from the cleaning agents used on them throughout their use.

Spoons

Wrythen twist

Diamond-top

Maiden-top

Acorn-top

1300–1600

Spoons were rare in the early Middle Ages but undoubtedly existed in wood, horn and other natural materials, and consequently have not survived. Not much is known about the development of the late medieval spoon but it is known they were personal possessions and often kept tucked in belts or hats. A person's social position was indicated by what type of spoon he or she carried. The poor had wooden, pewter or latten (a cheap metal to imitate bronze) the richer had fine pewter (see page 28) or silver, and many were personalised with initials carved into the back of a stem to discourage theft. Up to 1660, seal-top spoons were popular as these had a flat disc on top of the spoon, which could be etched with initials.

Knops vary and include a lion-sejant with shield, lozenge, pine-cone, seal top and animal head as well as those shown here.

From c.1400, maiden-head spoons appeared, sometimes with braided hair, a style restricted to married women; these may have been for a wedding trousseau. Apostle spoons becoame very popular from the 1500s when they were often given to children as christening presents and would represented their personal saint.

During the Commonwealth, apostle spoons declined (after 1650) as they were associated with Popery. The Puritan spoon was nothing more than the previous spoons with the tops cut off. Commonwealth Puritan spoons were the last to have a maker's mark in the bowl.

The placing of hallmarks on the back of silver spoons dates from 1300. Placed at the end of the stem, they are randomly arranged.

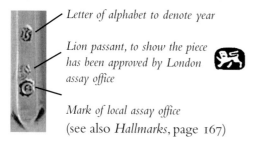

Letter of alphabet to denote year

Lion passant, to show the piece has been approved by London assay office

Mark of local assay office
(see also *Hallmarks*, page 167)

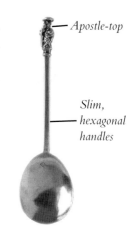

— *Apostle-top*

Slim, — hexagonal handles

Puritan spoon

Town mark is in the front of the bowl. Nearly all touch marks are small (0.40cm x 1.56cm) with well-made beaded circles. From 1650 they may be larger (1.5cm). 95 per cent of marks from 1650–1660 were circular, after which they are large ovals around 2.5cm high

Length: average 17cm
Materials: latten, (alloy of copper and zinc), pewter, silver, bronze
Bowl has very concave sides

Fig-shaped bowl

1600–1700

At the beginning of this century spoons popular from the previous era continued to be produced. Overall there was only one size of spoon – the tablespoon – made of a single piece of silver. The bowl was hammered in a die after the handle had been shaped, so expect to find slight variations in thickness. In 1670 two more spoons appeared: tea spoons – simply a smaller version of the tablespoons, approximately 13cm in length, and dessert spoons – slightly smaller than the tablespoon, which was then reserved for soup.

The materials are usually latten, pewter, silver, bronze and the average length is 10-20cm.

In examples from around 1680–90 the spoon terminal has a 'trefid' end, with two or three lobes. The name is a French term and comes from its resemblance to a three-toed doe's foot.

By *c.*1680, all hallmarks were on the back of stem, never in the bowl, as the blow from the punch dented the rat-tail. Generally there would be four marks, still arranged randomly.

Initials are often etched on the back. From *c.*1700 armorial crests appeared and spoons would have been laid face down so these decorations can be seen. To facilitate this, the terminal ends face forwards.

Around 1680, a short V-moulding at the junction of the bowl and stem gradually elongated to a rat-tail.

The stem became broader and flatter and more decoration, particularly on backs of bowls. The bowls themselves became more egg-shaped and deeper.

In around 1700, notches in the trefid became less pronounced, the central lobe was elongated and became known as 'dog-nose'. This style became very popular.

The end of the stem curves backwards, not forwards as spoons no longer had to be placed face down. However, this was uncomfortable to hold.

The dog-nose pattern coincied with the first time that sets of cutlery were laid out on a table in a set. Previously they had been individual possessions.

By 1710 the dog-nose was superseded by the Hanoverian, in which the handle is more narrow.

Hallmarks started to appear more regularly and grouped together. The bowl is also narrower, more like modern spoons.

1710 to date
Hanoverian, 1710–1780

From *c*.1710 the Hanoverian style became popular, called such because it was produced during the reign of George I, the first Hanoverian king. This design was common until *c*.1780 when it gave way to the simplified shape of the Old English.

It is characterised by a turned-up stem and a rib which runs from the base of the stem down about one-third of its length. Within the Hanoverian there are a number of sub-patterns.

Old English, 1760

The Old English pattern supplanted the Hanoverian in around 1760. It is very plain, with a more rounded end than the Hanoverian, and the rib in the former disappears. All cutlery was (and still is) placed face upwards so that the ends are turned downwards.

There are a number of sub-patterns such as Old English with Thread, named after the 'thread' that runs along the outside of the stem; and Old English Thread with Shell, in whichshell decoration was added.

Fiddle, 1775

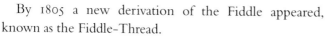

The Fiddle pattern evolved from Old English and differs in having 'shoulders', which give it its distinctive look. The name derives from its resemblance to the back of a violin. The Fiddle replaced the Old English pattern in popularity particularly during the nineteenth century, when it was used extensively.

By 1805 a new derivation of the Fiddle appeared, known as the Fiddle-Thread.

The Fiddle pattern is almost always accompanied by small protrusions near the bowl of a spoon or the tines of a fork.

With the Fiddle patterns a new technique was used, called 'double-struck'. This meant that the additional decorations, i.e. the thread or the thread and shell, appear

on both the front and back of the piece. These double-struck pieces are almost always heavier than single-struck ones.

1810 saw another derivation: the Fiddle-Thread and Shell. The more ornate the decoration the later the piece tends to be.

King's pattern, 1817

The King's pattern is a natural descendant of the Fiddle Thread and Shell and was popular during the Regency. There are about 20 variations of the pattern. The decoration is now much more extensive and continues further down the stem than the Fiddle Thread and Shell. It has a waisted appearance.

Queen's pattern, 1817

The Queen's pattern is distinguished from the King's in that the shell is convex; on the King's pattern it is concave.

Forks

Forks for eating came quite late to the table compared to the knife and spoon. Forks had been used previously but were reserved for serving and kitchen use. The earliest reference to forks being used for eating purposes is in a book of 1023, Hrabanus Maurus's *Glossiaria* which shows two men eating melon with large two-pronged forks. They were later introduced (c.1670) at a time when knives became blunter, to prevent (or at least minimise injury when) fighting at the table.

From the tenth to the thirteenth centuries, eating forks were common in Italy. However, many other European countries thought their use an affectation. In 1608 Thomas Coryate brought the fork to Britain despite being ridiculed. Early use of the two-tined fork, which was modelled on the kitchen variety, was primarily for sweet, sticky foods or for fruit which might stain the fingers. It was also used for pickles and current pickle forks retain this design. Forks changed very little and the two-tine example existed alongside, and was more popular, than the three- or four-tine version until the eighteenth century when the three-tine became more popular. The four-tine took over as the favourite in the nineteenth century.

c. 1550

Stylised terminals giving a flat surface for engravings are typical of this period.

Two fairly long, widely spaced tines ensure the meat would not twist while being cut.

Originally the points would have been sharp.

c. 1680

Blades became more curved to act more like a spoon, so one did not have to switch between the two

By *1680*, all marks appear on the back of the stem near the tines, never on the bowl.

c. 1750

Knives and forks were often kept in hard cases, as diners had to carry their own cutlery. The two were often made as a matching pair. The pistol handle fork (right) would match a scimitar knife.

Fork tines wear on the left side where they are more often in contact with the plate.

Late sixteenth century

In the late sixteenth century, the number of tines on forks increased to three or four. The extra tines made dropping food less likely.

Sharp tines scratched the soft pewter plates or tin-glazed plates and so become blunter. Silver forks are rare as they were often nicked by a sharp steel knife blade. Steel cutting edges were sometimes added to one tine to act as a blade for one-handed or disabled people. One belonged to Lord Nelson.

Hallmarks

Hallmarks were used to define the pureness of precious metals, where and when they were assayed (a confirmation that it reaches governmental criteria) and to denote the maker. Marks have never been more than five and are now four. The maker's mark and the date mark are not included here. Those included below are the main marks only and include the relevant dates.

The leopard head, the earliest hallmark, represents London as the mark of origin.

A: c.1300–1470
B: 1470–1515
C: 1558–92
D: 1681–9
E: 1719–40
F: 1756–1821
G: 1822–36
H: 1896–1916
I and J: 1916–to date

The lion passant represents royal control of the assay office and the standard of fineness in English silver (it was used for gold from 1544 to 1844).

A: 1544–50
B: 1550–58
C: 1558–1679
D: 1679–97 *After this the lion passant was replaced by the Britannia mark until 1719–39*
E: 1739–56
F: 1756–1822
G: 1822–96
H: 1822–96
I: 1896–1916
J: 1916 to date

The Civil War (1642-49) created such a demand for silver to pay the troops that afterwards coins (or clippings from the edges) were melted down to be remade into goods. As a measure to guarantee the purity of silver the Britannia Standard was introduced to ensure that the minimum silver content was 95.8 per cent. This hallmark of Britannia replaced the lion passant from 1697-1719.

A: 1697–1716
B: 1716–17
C: 1731–3
D: 1863–4
E: 1902

The Lion's Head Erased
A: 1710–11
B: 1717–18
C: 1725–31
D: 1726–7
E: 1863–4

Duty Marks are stylised portraits of the reigning sovereign to indicate that duty had been paid.

A: head of King George III (1760–1820) used 1784–6
B: head of King George III (1760–1820) used 1786–20
C: head of King George IV (1820–30) used 1820–30
D: head of King William IV (1830–37) used 1830–37
E: head of Queen Victorian (1837–1901) used 1837–90

Duty was abolished in 1890.

Hones or whetstones

Hones or whetstones (called so from the need to 'wet' the stone before use) do not appear until the advent of metals in the Bronze Age. During the Bronze Age a number of small 'hone' pendants are also made which may have been amulets or status symbols emphasising the importance of the new metal. Most tools and weapons need frequent resharpening, so hones were common, particularly during the medieval period.

They are made of a hard stone, and are specifically used for the sharpening of metal blades. There are many different types of stones used and a number of petrological studies have been done. Many are of local materials such as limestones and sandstones; however the most sought after were made of the micaceous schist first brought over by the Scandinavians in the tenth century. Schist from Norway came to be the preferred choice in hones from the eleventh century onwards and from the early to mid-fourteenth century it dominated the market. The principal quarry at Eidsborg, southern Norway, dates from the eighth century and exported to most of Western Europe. It finally closed in 1950.

Hones fall into two categories: those non-portable types fitted for workshops; and personal portable examples. Workshop hones are often of a coarser local stone, such as limestone or gneiss (a type of granite), than personal ones, and it may be that these were reserved for larger blades such as those used in agriculture.

Personal hones can be made from various materials and the coarser-grained hones tend to be wider and thicker than those of the smaller-grained schist and phyllite. The purple phyllite is a stone which probably originated from the Scottish highlands, Norway or Brittany. It is unclear whether the thicker examples were for larger blades or for initial sharpening, with the finer-grained versions being reserved for smaller tools and final sharpening.

Some are perforated for a thong to pass through for suspension from the neck or a belt. However, this hole is then a point of weakness and many are found broken across the hole. Alternatively, they may have metal covers attached to the top, such as that found at Llanbedr-goch, Wales.

The most common shape is a rectangle but size and form vary. Many have been worked into a longitudinal, or triangular, blunt point from sharpening on one or two faces.

The knife was drawn across the surface and scar marks may still be visible. Pins and needles were also sharpened using hones and the grooves they form may be seen. By studying the marks on the hone it may be possible to distinguish its use.

Bronze axes

Bronze axes first appeared in the Bronze Age. Initially they were cast in simple moulds of clay or in hollows in sand, making mass production possible. From 2000 BC they were also cast in open stone moulds. Axe shapes changed according to better hafting and casting methods. The harder iron eventually replaced bronze axes during the Iron Age.

Flat axe

The earliest of the bronze axes, these imitated the flint axes of previous eras and were probably hafted in the same way.

They were cast in one-piece moulds and ground with a whetstone (see page 169) to remove the 'flashes' or casting debris. Some examples may be ornamented with geometric designs.

Miniature flat axes also occur and were probably used as pendants.

The edge flares out as a result of being hammered to create a cutting edge and to harden the metal. If the hammering went too far the blade could crack and break, but it could always be re-melted.

©TT

Flanged axe

This was a natural development from the flat axe. It is still made in a one-piece mould but is of a more sophisticated design. It would have been hafted in a branch with a right angle that had been carefully selected .

The sides are hammered to make 'flanges' on either side so it may be mounted more securely in its haft. Hammering the two edges to a ridge makes the axe thinner and wider. The blade is still flared.

Palstave

This is made from a two-piece mould. A stop ridge has developed and it is this which distinguishes it from a flanged axe. The blade is narrower than in earlier axes.

The sides are no longer hammered, but are made as part of the casting process.

Winged Axe

The flanges are hammered over to form wings. The tool has a small loop to allow it to be tied onto the haft.

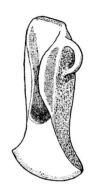

Socketed Axe

Socketed axes were made in a two-piece mould.

This was the height of the technology. It could be mounted on the strongest of handles and had ample bronze at the cutting edge and therefore lasted much longer before needing to be recast.

It has a hollow end, so the handle fits inside the socket.

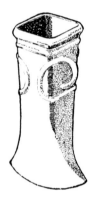

Roman leather shoes

Most shoes from any period are generally of leather. However other materials, such as fur, may have been used but have not survived. There are a large variety of shoes only a few of which are included here. There are four main types of Roman shoes: nailed, stitched, sandals and one-piece.

Nailed

Nailed shoes are made from a number of layers: the sole, one or more middle soles, the insole, heel stiffeners, and upper layers, which rarely survive.

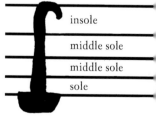

insole

middle sole

middle sole

sole

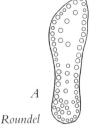

A
Roundel

Diamond

Leaf

'S' pattern

B

Soles

The sole (the layer in contact with the ground) consists of a thick piece of leather with, on the bottom, a number of iron nails. The nails serve several purposes; to attach the sole to the upper, to provide grip when walking and as reinforcement against heavy use. The nails in almost all British soles are curved (see picture on p172). When the Romans left Britain nailing in shoes ceased and did not return until Mark Isambard Brunel (father of Isambard Kingdom Brunel) designed nailed boots for the British army during the Napoleonic wars.

The use of separate soles meant that they could be replaced when worn, saving the cost of replacing the uppers, which generally used more leather.

There are three types of nailing patterns:

A: A single row of nails around the outside shoe edge, spaced approximately 15-25mm apart. Inside this row there are often groups of nails on the tread (ball of the foot), the waist and the heel. These groups vary but some patterning has been identified such as the roundel, diamond, leaf and 'S' pattern.

B: There is a single row outside the edge but the nails are more widely spaced than in type A. Internally there may be a line down the centre, or no additional nails at all.

C: Heavily nailed with at least two rows on the outside edge. Inside there is a series of closely spaced nails along part or all of the sole.

C

Insoles

These are roughly the same shape as the sole although they will be narrower and slightly smaller to fit on top of the sole. There are a number of slots a couple of millimetres in length and running at right angles to the shoe edge which allows for the tunnel stitching. These are spaced on average about 10–15mm apart. In the centre of the insole there are further thong slots 4–5mm in length and in pairs in the tread, waist and heel and at right angles to the horizontal shoe.

The middle soles are similar to the insole and have thong slots in the same position so they may marry. The middle soles may be several layers thick.

Thread was used on the uppers but on the soles rawhide thongs were used to provide more strength.

A military lattice, openwork Caliga. It would have had five-six soles with a single-piece upper sandwiched between them. Caliga as military wear lasted until c.AD 100. Non-military sandals have closer lattice-work

Uppers

Some uppers were made of goat and sheepskin but mainly cattle hide was used. They could have been a number of colours such as red, black, yellow, white or green, although in an archaeological context most colours have leaked out and the shoes are uniformly black.

Heel stiffeners

Stiff, crescent shaped pieces of leather used to reinforce the heel. They were nailed between the sole and middle or insole and the upper, so they have nail holes on the interior.

Stitched shoes

The uppers rarely survive so most evidence is from the sole, insole, middle soles and heel stiffeners. They are not nailed, with the exception of the attachment of the heel stiffener. Instead of nails the parts are stitched together using 'tunnel stitching' in which the thread is passed through 'tunnels' in the leather. The stitching passes in a serpentine pattern for a short distance inside the leather before emerging on the same side. The stitch therefore

Tunnel stitching

cannot be seen from the outside and is intended to make the shoe more waterproof.

Stitched soles have a series of holes running lengthwise near the edge, on the flesh side (rough side) and spaced roughly 10-15mm apart.

There are two kinds of sandals: the standard, which dates mainly to the first and second centuries, and the broad.

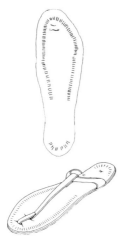

Standard sandals

Sandals consist of a sole that may have one or more middle soles and may have an insole. They may also be nailed. The soles are attached with thongs and the holes to allow for these can be seen in a series around the edges.

Sandals were traditionally worn in the house as it was considered impolite to wear street shoes inside. During the first century a divergence of styles occurred between women's and men's sandals. Men's tended to be rounded in the front while in women's sandals the toe tended to be more pronounced. They were generally made of softer materials and more brightly coloured.

Thong holes, about 2–5mm long. Additional holes are to be found near the toe to allow for the strap, which rarely survives

Broad sandals

Broad sandals appeared in the third century. The toe has widened out and is now wider than the waist. By the late third century some can be of enormous width, up to 150mm across and very triangular in appearance. The toe may be indented to follow more accurately the shape of the foot. The remainder of the shoe is of the same proportions as a standard sandal.

Drawings after Rhodes 1974

One-piece

The one-piece shoe is made from a single piece of leather held together by a seam at the back and laced over the foot. The term Carbatina seems to be a general term for a shoe that was cut so that loops in the upper could be threaded through with thongs and pulled tight. Some may have decoration, particularly on the heel, or may have openwork.

This type of shoe was among the earliest in the Greek and Roman worlds and continued into the medieval period.

Saxon and medieval shoes

The most common type of shoe in this period is the turn-shoe, a slip-on, low shoe or boot of about ankle length secured by a toggle-and-thong or tied-thong fastening. It lasted for about 1,000 years. They are called so because they were made in reverse and then turned inside out. The uppers were often made from one piece of leather although at times they were made in two parts, the vamp (the top part) and quarter (the back part). Even the quarters were occasionally made in two parts and stitched down the back. Also, rectangular or triangular inserts were sometimes added to alter the shape of the upper. Heel stiffeners were often added.

Turn shoe, a low slip-on shoe. Versions may be open or have laces fastened across the vamp or a strap and buckle

The uppers were then sewn to the edge of the sole using an edge seam with stitches that are small and closely spaced, approximately 5–7mm. Additional stitches were added to reinforce some areas and where the stitching was pulled tight there is often a wrinkling along the edges. The shoe was then turned inside out so that the grain side (smooth side) faced outwards and the stitching was not visible. This did, however, place stress on the leather and the stitching. Turnshoes were mostly plain but they could be decorated with openwork, embroidery, incising or engraving. In addition they would probably have been coloured, but most dyes will have been leached out in the soil. Repairs are common as is the cutting of the uppers to make a better fit. The shoes are presumed to be unisex but the shrinkage of leather makes it difficult to be certain of exact sizes. Uppers were made from a variety of leathers, including calf, sheep, goat and deer. The soles would have been from thicker leather, usually cowhide.

Turn boot, a low slip-on shoe. Versions may have the front fastened by a strap and buckle or laces. Alternatively the boot may have laces vertically down the side

A useful way of dating turnshoes is in the stitching. Saxons tended to use leather thongs for stitching, while later medieval shoes were stitched with thread.

The rand-shoe

One of the most important developments in shoe design in the thirteenth century was the introduction of the rand, although not all shoes of this date include it. They are extremely rare in early shoes but a shoe from the Sutton Hoo burial does include one. The shoe design remains more or less the same with the addition of a rand – a long, narrow, almost triangular, strip of leather that was inserted into a gap between the upper and the sole and sewn in place for a stronger, more waterproof join. The rand shoe still has to be turned inside out and stitch holes only appear on the inside of the sole.

The turn-welt shoe

The turn-welt shoe consists basically of a rand that has been enlarged to allow an extra sole or a repair sole to be added and acts as an intermediary between the turnshoe and the welted shoe.

The turn-welt has stitch holes visible on the grain side of the sole as well as the flesh side.

The welt is wider than the rand and has a double row of stitches.

Soles do not necessarily have to be of one piece. They are often made in two and the heel joined to the waist.

Upper

Stitch holes appear only on the flesh side of the sole

Rand

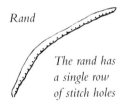

The rand has a single row of stitch holes

Upper

Stitch holes appear on both sides of the sole but only on the flesh side of the insole

Welt

The welt has a double row of stitch holes for both the sole and the insole

Pointed toe shoes

At the beginning of the twelfth century a new fashion for pointed toes becomes popular and remained so until the thirteenth century. The average length of the toe was approximately 10 per cent of the foot's length. Pointed shoes were really only ever worn by the aristocracy; the common people wore round-toed shoes or straight ones which could be worn on either foot.

Around 1140 the point curves, a style that lasted until the mid thirteenth century.

Pointed shoe

Very narrow waist

Small heel

Round-toed shoe

Straight shoe

Medieval leather shoes (c.1300–1450)

During the fourteenth century there was a greater standardisation of shoe design, and an increase in the use of smaller inserts to create more complex patterns and openwork designs.

The welted shoe

The final development of the rand/welt around 1500 culminated in the welt, which was placed on the outside of the seam rather on the inside. The direct result of this is that shoes no longer had to be turned inside out and heavier, longer-lasting soles could be attached to the shoe.
Like turn-welt, welted soles have stitch marks visible on both the grain and the flesh side. The stitches are larger, 6–10mm and 5–7mm apart.

Upper

Welt

Stitch holes appear on both sides of the sole. Stitch holes appear only on the grain side of the insole

Drawings after Rhodes

The pointed shoe

During the 1320s the pointed shoe's toes became very variable in length but generally they averaged about 20–40mm, although they could become very exaggerated, up to 60mm. In order to keep them stiff the ends were stuffed with moss, animal hair or wool. Laces were common in the fourteenth and fifteenth centuries and buttons appeared at the beginning of the fourteenth century, although they are not common.

Roman brooches

Most brooches were utilitarian and mass-produced, but they are rarely found in complete form; usually at least the pin is missing. Most date to the first and second centuries AD when brooches were fashionable. After the second century the range and number greatly reduce; the only brooch of note to remain is the crossbow, which is a marker of high status. Most are of copper alloy. Silver and gold are rare. Roman brooches can be split into three main types: safety pin, plate or disc and penannular.

Safety pin types

There are two techniques of tensioning the pin: sprung and hinged.

Sprung pin

The advantage of the sprung pin is that it spreads the tension so does not need to be as strong as a hinged pin. Sprung brooches are the most common in Roman Britain.

Hinged pin

The pin swings on an axis until restrained by a stop on its head.

Dolphin

This form is so named because it looks like leaping dolphin. It was very common in the first and second centuries.

They are simple bow brooches with some later hinged examples.

Sprung and hinged forms are found in south and midland England, petering out in the north.

They have a transverse head with short wings protecting the spring. The wings can in some cases be long and decorated.

The bow, which may have a beaded design along the back, can be square, D-shaped or V-shaped.

The catch-plate is small.

Dolphin

Trumpet, c.AD 45-second century

This is named after the shape of its head, which resembles a trumpet. It is among the best known, and is diagnostic of the Romano-British period. The finest were made of silver, sometimes gilt, and they were generally worn in pairs. They are rarely found outside Britain. Peak production was in the early second century.

The earlier versions have simple waist-knobs. Later versions have a waist-knob set between opposing acanthus leaves. These were very common in military areas and in the North in the first half of the second century.

Trumpet

Loop

Many Roman brooches were worn in pairs, one on each shoulder. They were attached to each other across the breast by a chain.

Fantail

Mid first to mid second century AD

It is named for its triangular foot. The most famous examples are those from Greatchesters, on Hadrian's Wall and from Tre'r Ceiri, Caernarfonshire.

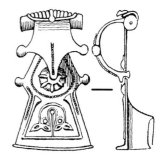

Fantail
Broad tail to the brooch
P-shaped profile

High arched, broad bow with ribs, pronounced knob and elongated foot

Aucissa, c.AD 50–65

Imported by Romans from the Continent, the aucissa is an early example of a hinged pin, sometimes on an iron axis. Occasionally the word *avcissa* or *atgivios* is on the head, assumed to be maker's name. It is well known on military sites from the whole of Britain but seems to have been replaced by British-made brooches.

Short, high arched bow, long catchplate and three onion-shaped knobs

Crossbow, c.early third-fourth century

The 'crossbow' is the most complex of Roman brooches. In early versions (*c*.200–50) the terminals were more bulbous and part of the bow and wing. In the fourth century the knobs became very large with some being screwed on. A hinged pin ran through the top of the bow holding the top knob in place. Crossbows were common on the Continent, but whereas most Romano-British types are solid, Continental versions tend to be hollow. The bow and catchplate could be elaborately decorated with incised patterns – ring and dot, lines, chevrons, spirals. They have been found made from most materials from bronze to gold, or gilded bronze in order to look like gold. Generally they are worn by high ranking males on the right shoulder with the top knob facing up. They appear often in Roman art.

Loop (see opposite)

Plate/disc types,
Second century AD to the end of Roman period

There is a huge range of these brooches, which were most popular during the second century. They are usually flat, but may have a domed centre, with a pin at the back, resembling modern badges. The decorations are frequently inlaid with enamel, glass, silverwork or semi-precious stone with colours that are normally red, blue, orange, green and yellow.

Fastened into projecting catch

Pins pivot in twin lugs on back of brooch, Some later types were sprung

The lmited space between plate and pin indicates expensive, lighter clothing

All ©PAS

Plate zoomorphic
Second–third century

Made in a number of designs, especially popular were dogs and hares (often running). Cockerels, dolphins, flies, birds, fish and horses were also common.

Animal brooches in particular are found on religious sites.

Horse and rider: Many found at temple sites, indicating a cult significance. Well known during second and third centuries.

Plate skeumorphic
Second–third century

Also popular are the skeumorphic (imitating an object) type. Popular are daggers, axes, soles of shoes, phalluses, swastikas, cornucopiae, wheels and chatelaines (right). They probably served as amulets, or lucky charms.

Dragonesque

These appeared in the late first century, were particularly popular in second century and continued into third century.

In the first century these consisted of a plain plate with two arms, one at the top for the hinge and another at the base to serve as a catchplate.

They were usually enamelled and very colourful and the patterns were derived from Celtic art.

They are found mainly in North Britain but exported as far as Hungary, France and Germany.

Copper-alloy cheap version

Silver, decorated version

Pennanular types
Iron Age onwards so difficult to date

A very common type, used for over 1,000 years. They consist of a broken hoop with a pin folded over the rim that can swivel around. Terminals are sometimes folded over or pinched in with simple designs, or are highly decorated, sometimes fashioned into animal heads. Terminals with elaborate zoomorphic designa began in late second century but were most popular in the fourth century.

Created by casting or from a bent rod, pins were made separately. The pin is humped or concave. A Roman pin is shorter than the Saxon version.

Roman zoomorphic buckles

Roman buckles were used predominantly by the army and can be seen on a number of tombstones and monuments. The zoomorphic copper-alloy Dolphin and Horse-head are probably the most distinctive.

Dolphin
AD 350–64

The Dolphin buckles are the most numerous among the zoomorphic buckles. The first types were copper-alloy cast in two parts, the loop and the pin. As these have no continental parallels they are accepted as being of British manufacture.

Their average width is *2.2–9* cm.

They consist of a sub-oval or D-shaped loop and may be decorated with punched dots or transverse grooving.

They depict confronting dolphins on the top of the loop with a bar or ball held between open jaws (upper left). Treatment of the dolphins is very varied: some are clear whilst others are simply stylised with a few incised lines (lower left). Some have upstanding crests like manes. The tails of the dolphins casn be either plain or decorated.

From *c*.AD 370 to the early fifth century a similar brooch was made but with horse heads.

There is a straight hinge bar onto which the pin would sit pointing up to the top of the loop. The pin, usually an inverted S-shape, rarely survives.

The buckle plate is a very distinctive long narrow strip of sheet bronze with a D-shaped, oval or rectangular loop, either plain or decorated, often with highly stylised dolphins.

The plate is doubled over the hinge bar and riveted with an iron stud.

There are holes to rivet the plate to a leather belt with iron studs.

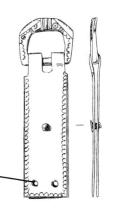

Fourth to mid fifth century and Anglo-Saxon imitations

A development of the dolphin buckle above was the three-part buckle consisting of the loop, pin and plate.

The loop is a confronting pair of dolphins similar to earlier Dolphin buckle. However, on the base of the terminals are hollow projections through which the bolt to attach the plate is passed through.

The average width is 2.4–5.6cm.

Open jaws with indentation where the pin rests.

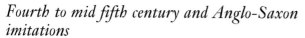

The tails on some loops are highly curved and the pin, when present, often has matching curved arms which interlock with the tails.

The pin terminal is doubled over to allow the bolt to be threaded through.

The plate when present often has four hollow cylindrical, decorated, projections at the top. The bolt passes through these, the two on the loop terminal and the pin, to attach all three pieces together.

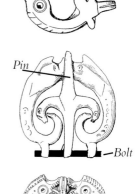

The average overall length is 3.7-6cm.

A number of holes are on the sides of the plate for iron rivets to attach to the leather belt

The plate is often openwork with three or four openings.

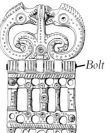

Rivet holes

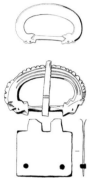

Late fourth to mid fifth century

A further development is similar to that above but the loop is cast in one with the plate so there are no in-curved terminals. An opening at the top of the plate allows a separately cast pin to be hooked though.

Continuing the derivative of the previous buckles, the plate now disappears and is replaced by two hinge bars.

The pin is attached to upper hinge bar and the plate to the lower bar.

There are no dolphins but stylised animal heads are now at the terminals of the loop, not at the top.

Fifth-century Anglo-Saxon brooches

Buckles now become semi-circular or D-shaped with a large loops terminating in open-jawed animal heads, often referred to as either lions or leopards, confronting across a hinge bar.

Most loops are plain but some are decorated with chip-carving, incised or stamped designs.

The plates are cast or sheet metal, folded double over the hinge-bar, semi-circular or rectangular in shape and riveted together. Most are plain but some have edge decoration.

Drawings after Hawkes
& Dunning 1962

Roman hairpins

During the first and second century the trend was for Roman women to wear their hair long, so a large number of long pins were required. Early pins tended to be crude and comparatively simple with a bulge in the middle and most bone examples would probably have been made at home. Examples from the later Roman period can be very elegant. During the third and fourth centuries, shorter hair was the vogue and this is reflected in the lower numbers of pins recovered.

1) Simple or plain pin, throughout Roman period

The top can be rounded or pointed with a plain tapering shaft ending in a point.

It is difficult to be certain about lengths as many pins would have been broken and then repointed so will appear shorter than the original.

The shafts are often smooth and well polished through use.

Length approximately 90-120mm

2) Transverse grooves beneath conical head c.AD 50–200

One to four grooves cut around the shaft below the head. The most common type has two grooves and the head can be elaborate or quite simple.

The grooves vary in depth and width and sometimes do not go all way around shaft.

Pins were made from a variety of materials such as bone, iron, bronze, silver and gold. However, the most common were of bronze or bone. Most Roman pins, no matter what the material used, share the characteristics outlined here. Bronze examples were generally cast and were more slender than those of bone. Often the head were decorated with a different type of material from the shaft such as jet, silver or pearls and would sometimes include busts of goddesses and empresses.

Pins were not necessarily used exclusively for the hair; they could have also been used to fasten clothing.

Length complete is roughly 70–125mm

3) Spherical or bulbous head, c.AD 200–400 or end of Roman period

The bulbous type has a variety of heads divided into four groups:

a) globular, elliptical, small flat area on top
b) semicircular, low convex upper half
c) lenticular
d) hemispherical.

Some faceting now appears.

Length approximately 50-110mm

Length approx 65–100mm

a) b)

Length 75-100mm

Lengths 65-83mm

Drawings adapted from Crummy 1983

4)Faceted, cuboid head c. AD 250–late forth, early fith century

This type is seen in metal as well as other materials such as jet. The head often has five sides with eight triangular facets but this is rarely achieved in bone due to the difficulty in carving. Bone examples appear in low numbers. Of those that do exist the faceting may seem irregular.

This kind of faceted cube can also be seen in beads of late third and forth centuries.

5) Reels beneath a conical or ovoid head, or cotton reel head, c.AD 250–late 4th, early 5th century

Similar to Type 2 but generally shorter and has one to five reels beneath conical or ovoid head. Generally divided into two groups:

a) unlike Type 2 in which the reels were cut into the shaft, Type 5 reels have been cut into a conical head

b) head and groove treated as two separate motifs (see below).

6) Reel- or bead-and-reel-shaped head or bead, reel and spool head. c.AD 250–late fourth, early fifth century

Most common is a solitary reel, often very roughly made in two types, the spherical head and the faceted cuboid head. In the fourth century, hair pins were both lathe and hand turned.

Other Roman pins include those that feature a human head, usually female. The head was made separately and then added to the shaft so that if the shaft broke the head could be attached to a new shaft.

Hair combs

Hair combs have been used since the Roman times not only for tidying the hair but also for the control of lice and dirt. They are usually divided into two types: one-piece or composite.

One-piece combs

One-piece combs are made from a single block of material such as bone, antler, ivory or various woods. Boxwood combs were common in the Roman period but were rare during Saxon times, when antler predominated. Boxwood then re-emerged in the medieval period, particularly the eleventh to thirteenth centuries, possibly because antler became rarer when deer become beasts of royalty (see antler page 45). The disadvantage of one-piece combs is that they are limited to the size of the antler or bone. This is particularly true of bone as it is difficult to align the teeth to the grain, which is necessary to give the teeth strength. Antler was much easier to use as it is possible to cut against the grain, and so many combs, often thought of as bone, are in fact antler.

Roman comb from excavations at Porchester Castle

Composite combs

Composite combs combine several pieces attached by iron rivets, though bronze rivets were also used. They are more difficult to make but last longer. Large numbers have been found from the Romano-British Iron Age to the medieval period The Romans particularly favoured long composite combs and these remained popular until the thirteenth century. Composite combs of wood or bone are rare and most are of red deer antler.

Antler composite combs date from the ninth–twelfth centuries.

Composite combs are further divided according to whether they are single-sided or double-sided. Single-sided were popular in the late Saxon period and included some triangular examples. Double-sided combs appeared around the eleventh century. They have tapering teeth in two directions, one side with finer teeth and the other with coarser.

Viking combs are found in great numbers and are common in graves. As they were owned by all ranks of society and carried at all times, it would have been easy to drop them. They are very similar in shape and method of production and identical examples have been found all over the Viking world.

Antler combs vary in size from 65mm long to very long ones of 30cm in length.

Composite combs consist of several pieces and were constructed in approximately five stages.

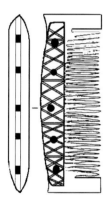

1) Two long back plates were cut from straight pieces of antler, preserving a slight curve. They range from plain to highly decorated, reflecting the wealth of the owner. Additional decorative motifs include ring and dot designs, slashes and cross hatching that are common on bone and antler items from the seventh century. The backs may also include bronze inlays.

2) A number of wider but thinner rectangular pieces were then placed between the back plates and riveted.

3) An iron rivet was usually placed on the seam between rectangular pieces.

4) The teeth were then cut with a fine saw into tapering points and filed with a fine file.

5) The projecting parts of the teeth plates were cut and sanded flush with the back of the comb, or left proud and decorated, such as the Viking comb on the front cover.

Those of the sixth to the ninth centuries are 'hog-back', or domed.

A rarer type is the Saxon handled comb. This consists of a handle of bone or antler with, at one end, the tooth segments. There are two types: the northern, which generally consists of a two-part handle that is secured along its length with rivets, and the southern, which is usually a shaped antler tine or cattle or sheep metapodial into which the tooth and end segments are inserted. They are then secured by iron rivets, after which the teeth are cut.

The bone examples generally date to mid Saxon whilst the antler examples appear more frequently in late Saxon.

Pilgrim badges

Pilgrimages began in the late twelfth century but most pilgrim badges date from the fourteenth–fifteenth centuries, the fourteenth being the heyday of pilgrimage. The most famous pilgrimage is Chaucer's *Canterbury Tales* written between 1387 and 1400. Thousands made pilgrimages every year with the more pious, or more adventurous, going to shrines abroad. The badge was a important part of medieval costume as it gave leave for the pilgrim to beg for alms and ensured a certain amount of respect; but it was, of course, also abused. The greatest pilgrimage was to Jerusalem, but other destinations included Rome, and the famous shrine to the apostle St James at Santiago de Compostela in Galicia, north-west Spain. Numerous items have been found along the known pilgrim routes which are still travelled today. A high number have been found in London, particularly from the Thames, and it has been suggested that pilgrims would throw them in as a votive offering, possibly to give thanks for a safe journey. Pilgrimages declined in popularity after the Dissolution of the Monasteries by Henry VIII in 1536–40.

Pilgrim badges, usually made by the monks, were easy and cheap to make so were produced in huge numbers for about 200 years. Most are made from pewter that was cast in moulds and some badges retain a pitted surface from being cast in stone moulds. Badges with a high tin content survive less well compared to those with a high lead content. Sometimes badges simply have holes so the item

could be pinned to clothing or hats; have loops or holes to be worn around neck; have pins at the back, or are charm-like, to attach to a chain.

The largest collections are in the British Museum and the Museum of London. The number of designs of pilgrim badges is vast and can sometimes be difficult to ascribe.

Many show figures of saints or apostles or images of religious significance. Shrines to the Virgin Mary often depicted the Madonna and Child, the Annunciation, or a crucifixion scene. The major shrines in Britain were Canterbury and Walsingham.

Ampullae

Ampullae first appear as early as the sixth century and were common to many shrines until the fourteenth century. They were usually filled with about a teaspoonful of holy water particularly from Canterbury where it was thought the water contained remnants of Becket's blood. The top of ampullae would be pinched tight to stop the water falling out and the vessel could be worn around the neck on cord passing through the two handles or loops or could be sewn on to something. Alternatively they could be hung up in churches. Pilgrims often sprinkled the water on the land and the ampulla was then buried in the soil. Some have holes where they were punched to allow the water out.

At the beginning of the fourteenth century pins and clasps were introduced as alternatives to ampullae.

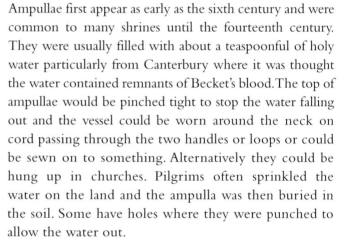

Canterbury

Thomas Becket was murdered at Canterbury in 1170 after a quarrel with Henry II, and was canonised in 1173. His was probably the most popular shrine until 1538 when Henry VIII declared him a traitor. Canterbury badges have a wide variety of designs (as would be expected in a 300 year period).

There are a great many designs concerning Becket and include the saint on horseback or on board ship to denote his return from his six-year exile in France, popular throughout the fourteenth and fifteenth centuries. A head and shoulders design wearing a mitre is probably the most popular. There is the letter T, or also a canopy or shrine.

Other badges show a reproduction of Canterbury bells.

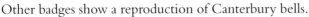

Walsingham

Walsingham, Norfolk, was popular in the fifteenth century for its shrine built in 1130 to the Virgin Mary and Christ. A common version of the pilgrim badge shows a shrine with Mary and Christ inside. Walsingham was also associated with ampullae, scallop shells, crowns, shields, flowers, initials and a crowned W. They are not as common as Canterbury examples.

Scallop shell

The scallop shell began as the icon of St James of Compostela but it also became accepted as a symbol of pilgrimage in general. Real scallop shells were often sold pierced to be worn around the neck.

Clay pipes

Early tobacco was exported from mainly Spanish-controlled America and, as Britain was at war with Spain tobacco was acquired with difficulty. Consequently tobacco pipes at this time are small. As tobacco became cheaper pipes got bigger. Tobacco was much stronger than today – about 10 times the strength – and was a narcotic and, during the plague (1665) it was believed, erroneously, that smoking prevented infection, so many people smoked pipes (and probably had cancer of the mouth!).

Pipes themselves were very cheap and were used much as cigarettes are today: once they were smoked they were thrown away, which is what makes them so ubiquitous in excavations.

c. 1580–1610

No, or rare, milling around rim
Small, 'acorn-shaped' bulbous bowl (approx 8mm)
Bowl is angled with stem
Small bore, approx 2-4mm
Stem straight about 100-160mm long
Heart-shaped, or flat heel.

c. 1610–1640

Milling around rim becomes common
End of seventeenth century a short, round spur is developed
Bowl becomes larger, approximately 13mm
Bore increases to 3mm
Stem becomes longer, approx 260-360mm

c. 1640-1710

Bowl sides become slightly straighter

c. 1680–1710

Milling becomes less common
Overall smoother finish, but bowl wall thinner
Top of bowl becomes parallel with stem
Stem more slender
Maker's mark appears on heel. Christian initial of maker on smoker's left side

From the first half of the seventeenth century, most makers' marks are on the heel.

From the second half of the seventeent century, maker's marks are on the stems or bowls. Stem marks date from c.1650 until the 1800s when initials were incorporated into the mould. Bowl marks (sometimes called a cartouche) are usually on the back. They are rare in the eighteenth century but were revived in the nineteenth century.

Use maker's marks with care because the same set can belong to a number of makers.

From the end of the seventeenth century until the third quarter of the eighteenth century marks are more commonly seen in the form of either a moulded cartouche on the right or left side of the bowl.

From the later part of the eighteenth century to the mid- nineteenth century pipes became more decorative in shape, influenced by the meerschaum. The whole bowl was made into heads of royalty, famous figures, and motifs.

Other changes included the length of the clay stem. It was popular at this time to have longer, exaggerated stems as this cooled the smoke before it reached the mouth. In the eighteenth century the Alderman, with a stem a foot and a half in length, was common. The longest in common use was probably the Churchwarden with a stem of almost two feet.

Clay pipes began to decline in popularity in the late nineteenth century when snuff became popular. They lasted until cigarettes appeared, *c.*1856, but cheap cigarettes finally saw them off after the First World War.

Dice

The popular vision of dice is small, six-sided cube of ivory, bone, wood (wooden dice were common in the eighteenth century and until the invention of plastics) or metal, although many other materials have also been utilised. They are used primarily in gaming. Each side of the die is marked with a number of incised dots or 'pips', or dots and rings. In most dice the opposite sides will always add up to seven; this has been a tradition as far back as Roman times and seems to be common throughout much of the world.

During the Romanised Iron Age and later, a distinctive type of dice was used known as the Parallelopiped. These

were popular on the Continent and used in Britain for a long time. They disappeared in Southern Britain when the Romans arrived and was replaced by the six-sided cube. However, in Northern Britain they were to last for several hundred years.

These dice have long parallel sides, and are essentially hollow tubes. The values are placed irregularly along the length.

Obviously, these cannot be rolled and their use is not exactly known. It is believed they were simply thrown down.

Prior to the introduction of dice in Roman times, knucklebones were used. These were usually the ankle bones of sheep. They had dedicated games themselves and continued in existence after dice came into use. A popular game was to toss five into the air and catch them on the back of the knuckles – hence the name.

Early Roman *tali* dice from the first century are believed to have been modelled on knucklebones. The values on the dice correspond to the values in the game of knucklebones.

Later dice, called *tesserae,* are squarer and and many are made from the shafts of small long bones, such as the metapodials of sheep. Often the ends would be open and were either used as four-sided dice, in which case the values 1 and 2 are usually omitted, or a small piece of bone was inserted into the top and the values added. Dice made from alternative materials such as antler, although solid, can still have the values 1 and 2 omitted. When all sides have values, opposite sides will usually add up to the traditional 7, although there are exceptions. The values are often represented with a dot-and-ring design and whilst size can vary the average size is about 1cm square.

Some dice can be very crudely made and these were probably made at home.

Viking and Anglo-Saxon dice

Dice were predominantly made from antler as it is easier to carve (see page 43) although as in other periods they were also made from bone, ivory (particularly walrus ivory) jet, wood and horn, although the last two have not survived well.

Viking and Anglo-Saxon dice differ from Roman ones in that they are often rectangular (similar to the parallelop-iped) with, on the long sides the values of 3, 4, 5 and 6 with the 1 and 2 on the short ends. Standard versions of dice also existed but the opposing values do not always add up to 7.

Both Roman and Anglo-Saxon dice have often been x-rayed and a number have been found to contain small weights internally, showing that loaded dice have a long history!

Medieval dice

Medieval dice are, for the most part, cubes like those of today, but opposing sides do not always add up to seven.

Parallelopiped dice were still common in the twelfth cen-tury and are rectangular dice that are long rods with, on the long sides values placed irregularly along the length. The small ends are no more than half or two thirds the length of the longer sides. It is not known how these dice were used but when recovered they are often found in sets of two and three.

A hoard of medieval dice was recovered from the Thames and are now in the Museum of London which. Upon x-ray they were found to be weighted with small pieces of lead.

Dice thereafter changed very little.

Modern dice

Medieval keys

Locks were custom-made for specific pieces of furniture and early versions were therefore expensive.

There are two types of locks used: lever and tumbler.

Lever locks were used from the thirteenth century. A key was turned to push a spring out of the way and move the bolt aside. Lever lock keys are easily recognised by their distinctive wards.

Tumbler locks appeared in the nineteenth century and consist of a perforated metal bolt, which unlocked when a suitable key was inserted to lift vertical pins out of bolt. They were usually made from iron.

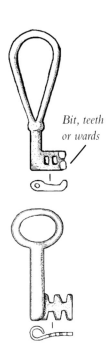

Bit, teeth or wards

1) *Eleventh century until end of the twelfth*

The earliest keys are characterised by a high loop-shaped bow. The bow can be circular but these tend to be towards the end of this period. The shank is hollow in order to fit into a pin in the lock.

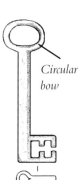

2) *Late eleventh–thirteenth century and later*

The bow is usually circular or oval. By thirteenth century the most common bow is round or oval with a straight, plain shank. Instead of being filed, wards are roughly cut with a chisel. The shank and bit are rolled out of single sheet.

3) *Early twelfth century*

Represented sporadically throughout the Middle Ages and comes in variety of shapes and sizes. St Peter was a popular figure in medieval times and is often represented in art carrying a key of this type. This differs from the keys above in that the bit is of a more solid construction. It is no longer rolled out but made separately and welded into place. However, it is still intended to fit a projecting pin, so the shank is hollow.

Circular bow

4) *Common twelfth–fifteenth century*

This is a new development in key design and has the distinct advantage that it can, for the first time, be used from both sides of the door. By the late twelfth century, the tapered end of the shank has decreased and in the fifteenth it rarely projected below the bottom of the bit. However, during the fourteenth and fifteenth century the shank lengthened again.

The shank is solid with tapered end.

More heart shaped bow

5) Thirteenth–fourteenth century

These lozenge-shaped bows, with or without protruding lobes were common in the thirteenth and fourteenth century, usually on chest or casket keys.

Toothing appeared along the fore edge of the bit in the late twelfth century but did not become fashionable until the thirteenth century. It appeared on chest keys in the fourteenth century.

6) Thirteenth–fifteenth century

The bow may be circular but more often oval or kidney-shaped. The circular form dates from the mid-thirteenth century while the kidney-shape is characteristic of the fifteenth century.

Solid stem narrows to a point.

This type was very common in the fifteenth century. It is usually made of iron.

The bit is symmetrical.

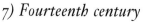

7) Fourteenth century

Solid shank, bored at end to form conical hole.

This type has a more elaborate lobed or lozenge-shaped bow. Occasionally the lozenge has angles like that of type 5. The lobed bow is characteristic of the fourteenth century. Occasionally there is a loop on top for suspension.

The bit is massive.

8) Fourteenth–fifteenth century

Similar to Roman and Viking.

9) Fifteenth century but majority post-medieval.

The shank may be tubular and open at the end or solid. It was used for chests rather than doors.

From the fifteenth century onwards keys tended to be made in steel and can be masterpieces. They were forged, chiselled and turned on a lathe.

Drawings adapted from the *London Museum Medieval Catalogue*.

Seal matrices

Seals are images and legends carved into a matrix in order to produce a positive impression that will be durable. They existed during the Roman period but in the intervening period until the eleventh century they were the preserve of the rich and powerful. It is not until the end of the twelfth century that general bureaucracy increased and with it the need for documents. In a time when the majority of people were illiterate seals were then widely used. Many could be bought at local fairs but these were mass-produced and contained little personal information. Also, these ready made seals often contain mistakes, abbreviations or local vernacular. Alternatively seals could be custom made in which personal details were generally included. These took the form of initials, names or designs. It is these smaller, personal, or mass-produced seals, which are commonly found. Larger seals from corporations and governmental offices tend to be kept.

Although most seal matrices are of metal they can be made of other materials such as baked clay (like the cylindrical seals of the Assyrians), lead, ivory, stone and wood. They are used primarily to impress a mark into wax to prove a durable record of ownership or authority in place of a signature. They also serve to secure contents against unauthorised opening.

When an owner died or had no more use for the seal it was usually destroyed or defaced to prevent use by anyone else. There are five basic kinds:

Single seal

The single seal is the most common.

Material

During the eleventh century, ivory and jet were used, but by the twelfth and thirteenth centuries the most common materials are lead, copper alloys and silver.

Lead was cheap and easy to engrave and was common among poorer people but is rarer after the early fourteenth century. The most common shape of lead seals is circular or vesical. The majority of medieval seal matrices are made of latten (see p 21).

The engraving is usually of a higher standard in these copper-alloy examples, particularly in the later period, and there is also far more variety shown in the choice of motifs and design.

Shape

A number of shapes are known, including circular, triangle, square, oblong, diamond, hexagonal, octagonal, shield-shaped, lozenge-shaped and the most common, the vesica (pointed oval). Sixteenth and seventeenth-century seals changed greatly in shape and style.

©PAS

At the apex is usually a cross, star or other small design.

Legends begin on the left-hand side (the right side on the impression) and often begins with an S, an abbreviation of the Latin *sigillvm* or 'seal'. Other versions may be *sigil* or *sig*.

Certain letters may have a line or stroke through them or, an apostrophe after them to denote the word has been shorted to save space. The Christian name then follows.

After this is the surname.

Personal names

Surnames generally did not become common until the thirteenth century. Instead many people were recognised by their relation to their father, and seals reflect this. Often Christian names are followed by the Latin *filivs* or *filia* to signify a son or daughter respectively, which may be shorted to *fil'*. Another way of distinguishing male and female names is by the suffix *i* for male and *e* or *ae* for women. Women's names tend to be found on lead seals and less frequently on bronze ones.

Seals with personal names generally date from the thirteenth and fourteenth centuries; after this personal names on seals decrease in favour of stock legends.

Legends

For those who could not afford to have seals made personally many could be bought ready made and certain words and inscriptions appear regularly:

Secreti: secret or secretia: secrets.

Prive: private

Ave Maria Gratia Plena: 'Hail Mary Full of Grace'; popular in the thirteenth century.

Ecce Agnus Dei: 'Behold the Lamb of God'; popular in the thirteenth and fourteenth centuries.

In the fourteenth century mottoes relating to romance appeared for sealing letters and may be accompanied by appropriately romantic imagery.

By the sixteenth century there are few legends, as they were replaced by simple initials which were often bought ready-made. Roman lettering also increased in popularity during the sixteenth century.

Roman

Roman lettering (twelfth century and sixteenth century)

LOMBARDIC

Lombardic (late twelfth century with the occasional mixture of Lombardic and Roman styles)

BLACK LETTER

Black letter, c.1350. By this time medieval French and English are employed as well as Latin.

Merchants' Marks

Merchants' marks appeared around 1330 and early ones are often accompanied with a flag and cross. By the fifteenth century they became simple in design and many simply have initials or crowned initials. By the sixteenth century the use of seals by merchants has decreased.

Images

Until the advent of popular seals, most seals were used by royalty and the Church and as such many included images of kings and popes. Early seals copied this iconography and in the eleventh century would often feature the head and shoulders of, usually, a saint. Often in early seals the legend related to the image.

©PAS

Designs for the central panel varied widely but recurring themes were the fleur de lys, and flowers with four or eight petals.

By the end of the thirteenth century the designs were becoming larger and more ornate, with few empty spaces left, and by the fourteenth century the seal was often filled with heraldic imagery.

©PAS

However, a change then took place and more personal images began to appear particularly for use on letters. Images were used in association with hearts and flowers or clasped hands.

Seals range in size from 2cm to 4cm in diameter.

Single seals can be of a piece of flat metal with tab at the top to serve either as a loop for carrying or for lifting off the impression. The back is plain (see middle picture).

©PAS

Seals from the late twelfth century can also have a lug on the back, centrally placed, or near the edge. The handles very in size and form but generally the late twelfth century examples are larger than those of the thirteenth century.

Double seal

A double seal is made of two pieces of flat metal both of which are engraved. On the corners are between two and four lugs to hold the two together.

Ring

Intaglio matrices can be as small as 2.5cm, often made from semi-precious stones. Set into rings or fobs they can be double or single-sided. Carnelian, a dull red semi-precious

©TT

stone, was often used. Many become part of a finger ring.

Pendant

Pendant seals began to appear in the late thirteenth century and continued in use until the end of the fifteenth century. The majority are made of copper-alloy although some rare examples are known in silver. It is unusual to find anything other than a round matrix but the heater shield shape is known for the armorial type. They all have a hexagonal or round handle which tapers to a pierced terminal of circular, lozenge or quatrefoil form. Occasionally examples are found with a suspension chain or the rusted remains of one still attached . Leather thongs or laces may also have been used.

Pendant seals appear to become popular again in the seventeenth century. They are depicted in contemporary paintings of the sixteenth century and so it may be that this form of seal though less widely used could have survived through to the later period.

Desk Seals
Seventeenth century
Desk seals were popular during the Tudor period and by 17th-18th centuries had wide spread use.

Fob seals
Eighteenth century
Fob seals are made of various metals. By the late eighteenth century they are very ornate. Some fobs have four or five seals attached. Many were mass produced ready-made seals.

Horseshoes

The first written record of iron horseshoes is in AD 910. However, it is not until the Crusades (1096-1270) that shoeing becomes important, when iron had become cheaper and more plentiful. The Crusaders rode to battle on large Flemish horses. However, damp northern latitudes tend to make horses' hooves soft with wear so they need to be shod regularly. The shoes had to be removed periodically to cut the growing hoof and the same shoe was often replaced until worn or lost. Iron would have been reused so most horseshoes found today would have been casually lost.

Most are found in a highly corroded state and can only be recognised by their distinctive curving shape. For more details they will usually need to be x-rayed.

Medieval horses were much smaller than those of today. The overall hoof size was 90-115mm whereas a modern horse's hoof is between 120-140mm.

Tenth to twelfth century
Wide-webbed but thin (approximately 3-4mm) crude in appearance, overall width of about 100mm.

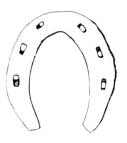

The nail-holes are circular with rectangular counter sinkings, to hold and protect the head of the nail, formed by using a punch.

A horseshoe is in the shape of a keyhole, the inside being where the 'frog' of the hoof would be.

There are three nail-holes of around 7-8mm diameter in each branch .

Eleventh–thirteenth century
The webs are narrower than in early types and slightly thicker (approximately 5mm). The overall width is about 102mm but rarely exceeds 110mm

Between 1250 and 1320 horses were being used on farms in greater numbers than the traditional oxen.

There are deep oval or rectangular nail holes. Punching in the holes pushes out the rim to form typical 'lobate' profile.

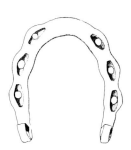

There are still usually three nail holes in each branch, but occasionally four.

Shallow calkins may be present.

Calkins are a regular feature on about 90 per cent of horseshoes and appears in four formats:

1 thickened heel

2 right-angle

3 folded

4 double-folded

—*Calkin*

Thirteenth–fourteenth century

These return to a wider web, and are generally heavier averaging *108*mm in width.

However, this type had a relatively short life, being typical of the second half of the thirteenth century and the early fourteenth century. The type has smooth edges.

Calkins are less common than in the eleventh to thirteenth centuries but still account for around 78 per cent. Folded calkins are the most common.

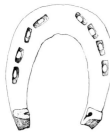

From the thirteenth to fourteenth centuries, shoes could be bought ready-made with rectangular nail-holes.

The margin between holes and the edge is sometimes quite broad.

There are often four holes on each branch or four on one and three on other. As it was believed the outside edge would wear quicker than the inner.

Fourteenth–sixteenth century

These have wide webs with no countersinking around the holes, but are more square or rectangular. On average square holes outnumber rectangular.

Can have *3 / 3* holes, *3 / 4* or *4 / 4* on the branches.

Fewer calkins are present, about 56 per cent. The folded kind is now rare with the norm being right-angled or thickened.

In the seventeenth century and later, horseshoes were large and heavy, and had more nail-holes which are spaced right around the shoe, including the toe. Holes are now punched through a fuller (a longitudinal groove) which was introduced in the first half of the nineteenth century and worked on the same basis as the counter sinkings, to accommodate the nail and protect the head of the nail.

Modern horseshoe showing the central fuller groove.

In the eighteenth century Industrial Revolution, horses were used extensively and huge numbers of horseshoes were made. As transport improved horses became redundant in the workplace.

Donkeys, mules and oxen have also been shod from the earliest times. Donkey and mule shoes do not have the keyhole shape of a horseshoe; they are longer and narrower with fewer holes, usually two on each branch.

Spurs

Spur became a popular fashion item worn by both men and women. In fact a person's position in society could be ascertained by the type of spur he wore. A knight would wear gold, or gilt, an esquire (upon becoming an esquire spurs were presented to him thereby 'earning his spurs') silver and a page tinned. Spurs were often buried with their owner.

The spur was attached to the foot with two straps – one running under the foot, the other over the instep – secured to the spur by metal hooks that clipped on to rings on the terminal end of the spur. There are two basic types of spurs, the prick and rowel.

Roman

The earliest spurs are those found in Etruscan tombs of the second century BC and the Roman versions are similar. Made of bronze, they were of simple design with short rounded sides less than 60mm thick and a spread of 640mm wide. They have a single central protrusion, or goad, round in section and about 160mm long. On the end of the terminal is a button over which a strap would be fitted. This design was not to re-appear until the late eighteenth century. A later design of Roman spur had rectangular terminals about 130mm wide with slots cut into them, into which a strap was threaded and are similar to those found in the Norman period. However, Roman examples are identified by the spike. Roman spurs rarely exceed 250mm. They have been found at a number of sites in Britain such as at Hod Hill, Dorset.

Prick spurs

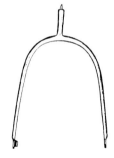

Prick spurs were made up until the around 1300 when the rowel was introduced. The goad (prick) began as a simple tubular point (Type a) used from Viking times onwards. From the eleventh century Type b was popular and up to c.1100 the goads are simple and small, after which they become larger. Goads have many shapes but the most common are the four (Type e) or eight sided pyramid type (the later from the eleventh century), a pointed cone type, and a shape usually rounded in cross section. The prick is riveted though the heel of the spur.

The neck was long and blunt, about 500mm long and round in section with a flat end into which the spike was inserted.

Points

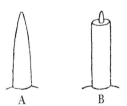  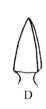

| A | B | C | D | E | F |

Ninth and tenth centuries

During this time, a new type of point, the ball and spike, was developed to prevent the goad entering the horse. Usually made of iron, or gilt iron, they had slender sides, slightly curved in triangular section. The terminals ended in small knops from which the spike protruded. The necks were 380mm long, 160mm thick, and slightly curved downwards (usually riveted on). The ball was usually oval, 190mm long, 160mm thick, with a short spike of about 130mm long. The surface of the ball may show hammer marks. The ball was close to the heel of the spur which had no neck.

Effigies of Henry I and Richard I both show ball and spike spurs.

Ball and spike terminal

Terminals also appear in a variety of forms:

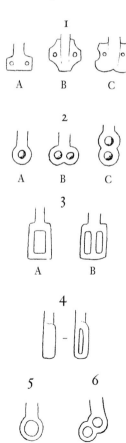

Type 1 is the earliest, from the tenth century. These early spurs had leather straps riveted to the spur terminal.

Type 2 terminals became circular. Prior to *c.*1100 there was as many as two (c) to six rivets. Between *c.*1100 and *c.*1250 just one large rivet is common (a). From *c.*1100 to *c.*1250 there are some spurs that have two slots on each arm.

Type 3. This is used like a figure 8 terminal so that a wide strap goes through the slot and attaches to the leathers.

Type 4 is a rarer slot form.

Type 5 appears after *c.*1250 with a single large loop

Type 6 From around *c.*1350 to about *c.*1425 the terminals became a matched pair of single holes loops resembling a figure of 8. This was most common on bronze spurs from *c.*1350 to about *c.*1380 and seen less frequently after that. The strap was attached via spur hooks that clipped into the loops.

During the thirteenth and fourteenth centuries there was also a combination of terminals with, on the one arm a loop and the other a slot (see below). This would allow the strap to be pulled tight to the foot. Most of the early rowel spurs had this arrangement.

Until around 1150 spurs had straight sides (see picture of prick spur on page 207). After this they became curved around the ankle (this continues for as long as prick spurs are used). Most were made from iron, and were tin-plated to give a silver appearance.

Rowel spurs

Prick spurs fell out of use between c.1300 and c.1325 and, with a few exceptions, did not show up again until after 1800. Rowel spurs started to appear shortly before c.1300 but are rare and they did not become standard until 1325.

Made of copper alloys and iron, rowel spurs were probably both cast and forged. Sometimes they had gilt, were enamelled, or tinned. Spurs with carved decoration were almost always made of a gilt copper alloy.

Early rowels are much like prick spurs with the characteristically strongly depressed sides that curve under the ankle bone, as seen earlier.

For a short time in the late fourteenth century there was a very distinctive type of spur where the arms curve down, back up, then plunge downwards again at an almost 90° angle.

Rowels were sharp, pointed wheels, sometimes decorated and generally were less harmful to the horse than the prick spur.

Between around 1370 and 1410 spurs could have a large number of points (12 to 32) and rowels are divided into 'star' points, those whose points are divided right up to centre, and 'rose' points when the points are divided only part of the way. The term 'folliated' points usually means rowels of other designs.

Rowels are usually around 380-510mm in diameter and sat at the end of a neck (approx 510mm long) fitted into a

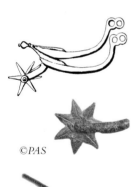

©PAS

©PAS

slot at the end of the spur arms in order for them to rotate.

During the fifteenth century, spurs with necks of extraordinary length appear. They developed in response to designs in horse armour and needed to reach around the heavily armoured flank. They could be worn either inside or outside the wearer's armour with the neck protruding outwards. The neck is often over 25.40cm long with the entire length of the spur being 27.94-35.56cm.

Representation of rowel spurs on a contemporary brass of Sir Thomas le Strange (died 1426 at Wellesbourne Hastings), Warwickshire from Medieval Catalogue

Thimbles

From prehistoric times people have used some hard item to protect their fingers whilst sewing. Mammoth ivory (see page 47) was used to aid in applying pressure whilst stitching using needles of bone, or wood or other hard materials. Metal thimbles were not required until the use of steel needles developed in the eleventh century. The earliest thimble is from China from a tomb dated *c.*206BC-AD 220. It is thought that the first thimbles in Europe were brought back in the fourteenth century.

Hispano-Moresque

These date to twelfth–fifteenth century with little subsequent change in shape.

Cast in one piece in copper-alloy, they tend to be heavy and approx 5cm high.

They have short, straight side but no rims, and may have some decoration. The base is an irregular circle.

With a distinctive 'bullet'-shape, tops can be rounded or pointed with bare crowns.

Indentations, or knurlings, are large and round as this kind of thimble was probably made for heavy work with

large needles. They are referred to as 'waffle-shaped', which means the knurlings are quite square.

Acorn cup, beehive or skeps

These date from 1300 to 1450 but are difficult to date precisely.

Knurlings are hand punched, and are low and irregular. They start from the bottom and work up towards the crown.

Either cast or hammered into a die, the acorn cup was made from copper and copper alloys, but a high copper content caused a discolouring of the fingers and clothing. For hammered examples look for fold marks.

The acorn cap is fairly shallow and sometimes has a hole in top, possibly caused by casting process.

Acorn

Levantine

Ninth to eleventh centuries.

Introduced into Europe by the Crusaders, they are the only thimble to bear a chevron or cross.

Levantine

Medieval

Fifteenth to sixteenth centuries.

The regular open indentations present indicate that larger needles were being used. They are still being cast or hammered, but are deeper in shape and still rimles.s

Early silver thimbles do not have a hallmark as they weighed less than the statutory five pennyweights.

Medieval

Nuremberg

Mainly sixteenth century.

They have a tall slim body, widening towards the base and little decoration until the sixteenth century. More intricate decoration is common on Nuremberg examples.

Caps were soldered on and have a flattish top. Knurlings are still hand punched, forming a spiral, winding up the sides and continuing over the top. Their fineness is a sign they were used for fine needles.

Nuremberg

A large number of companies began making Nurembergs. Maker's marks sometimes appear at the beginning of the knurlings.

Thimble technology was improved in around 1530 in Nuremberg, Germany, when makers were able to produce sheets of uniform thickness, colour, consistent quality and greater comfort. Made mostly of copper and zinc, they were a bright colour for the cheaper market, whilst silver was popular for those who could afford it as it does not mark the thread. Nurembergs were a great success and exported worldwide; they dominated the industry during the middle and late sixteenth century.

The greater consistency allowed more flexibility in design and decoration. Filigree, an open-worked cover slipped over a smooth body, first appeared in the sixteenth century. At the end of the century toy or miniature thimbles were introduced; they were intended as gifts rather than having any functional purpose.

From the seventeenth century onwards, thimbles become squatter in shape and standardised in form. Plain examples can be difficult to date.

In the nineteenth century, industrialisation led to a greater range of fabrics and a greater demand for thimbles. By Victorian times they were being machine made and the knurlings became very regular. A band also appeared at the base to prevent injury if the needle slips. Most thimbles prior to the nineteenth century were made of copper alloys or precious metals. The introduction of steel (see page 36) made this a common metal for thimble manufacture. However, steel thimbles are susceptible to rusting.

Pin beaters

The pin beater was a multi-use tool for the weaver. Made of bone, antler or wood, the pointed ends were used to pick and push errant threads into place and keep everything equally spaced. They can be divided into three basic types:

Cigar-shape

This first appears during the Roman period and continues in use until the Norman Conquest, when it seems to have disappeared from use at the same time as clay loomweights. They are evenly polished all over from wear and have two working ends.

The band of incised marks in the centre gives a better grip.

Flatter form

This has a pointed working end and a butt end which can be oblique or chisel shaped. It is smooth all over but wear seems to be concentrated in the centre and the pointed end. It is held with the butt end in the palm. They date between the late ninth, early tenth and the fourteenth centuries. They are usually 80-150mm long.

Curved

Longer than the others – up to 170mm in length. Rounded in section with a lengthwise curve. Wear is concentrated in the centre and at the pointed end. Date from the ninth to the twelfth century.

Spindle whorls

Spindle whorls (once called pixies' grindstones in folklore) are small, circular discs with a central hole. They were threaded onto a spindle, a thin wooden stick, in order to spin wool and flax. It was a simple task done by women and children and one that could be undertaken whilst doing other jobs such as watching animals. The spindle was small enough to be tucked into the waist and probably many were lost in this way. Consequently they are found in many locations.

A spindle whorl needs to be made to specific requirements. It needs sufficient weight to make the yarn stretch and to make the spindle spin and keep a regular momentum. It needs to be of convenient size to fit into the hand and the hole must be made to fit the spindle tightly.

They can be of many materials, such as reused pottery sherds, local stones such as limestone or chalk, bone, antler or lead. Stone whorls were often lathe cut whereas softer materials such as limestone could be cut with a knife and marks may still be seen. Bone whorls, though never as common as stone ones, were often cut from cattle femurs (cattle until relatively recent times were smaller than modern ones) as it was a suitable shape and only needed some knife trimming to make it usable. Other bone examples are from pig femurs which, given their smaller size may have been for use by children. Bone was used over a wide period of time but it is most common in late Anglo-Saxon to early Anglo-Norman times. Antler, used from Roman to medieval times, were cut from the antler pedicle (the part of the skull where the antler rises). Lead examples were made from Roman times onwards and would have been cast in moulds. Decoration on lead whorls tends to be from the late medieval or Tudor periods and ranges from ring and dot marks to more elaborate patterns.

Sizes vary; the larger and heavier examples may have been for heavier yarns. There are a number of standardised sizes.

Roman whorls range from 2-5cm in diameter with a characteristic hole of 5-7mm in diameter.

Single flat face: ninth–twelfth century

Two flat faces, one larger than the other: ninth–tenth century

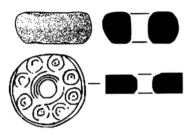

Two flat faces both equal; eighth–early twelfth century

No flat faces. Typical of medieval northern and eastern Britain of the twelfth–fourteenth century

All of the four types shown have a standard size hole of 9-11mm.

Sizes vary but can be classified approximately:
Those made from medieval cattle femurs are approximately 35-50mm diameter.

Stones ones are approximately 28-40mm.

Ones from pig femur approximately 20-30mm.

As with modern cotton reels, whorls usually have a cut to secure the thread somewhere on the top.

Warp weights disappeared at the end of the fourteenth century except in poorer places, which would have kept the warp loom.

Bone skates

Bone skates are frequently found items. They have a long history : some dating from 3000BC have been found in a lake in Switzerland. They occur throughout the world. The Romans had them as did the Vikings but most of the evidence dates from the twelfth century when the first literary reference was made to them:

Others are more expert in their sports upon the ice: for fitting to and binding under their feet the shinbones of some animal, and taking in their hands poles show with iron, which at times they strike against the ice, they are carried along with as great rapidity as a bird-flying or a bolt discharged from a cross-bow (from Reader 1910).

Most skates are the meta-carpals or meta-tarsals of horses and oxen (in Dutch the word for skate is 'schenkel' which means 'leg bone') and would have been cheap to make, probably being made at home. They would have been difficult to manoeuvre as they lack an edge which is needed to launch the foot from the ice. Consequently skaters needed to use a pole to propel themselves along the ice, as mentioned in the quote above. In the fourteenth century, the Dutch were using wooden skates with flat iron runners but they still needed to use a pole for propulsion. Metal skates appeared in the fifteenth century, and a 1498 woodcut shows metal blades. Both metal and bone skates were used contemporaneously, probabecause metal skates were expensive. In the sixteenth century the Dutch added a double-edged metal blade to the wooden skates, which meant the pole could be abandoned as there was now leverage on the feet. It was not until the late nineteenth century that skates were attached to the boot.

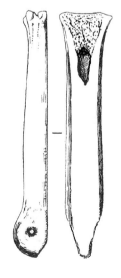

Holes are drilled at one, or both ends to allow for leather straps to hold the skate over the shoes.

They are characteristically polished smooth on the lower surface in order to glide better. They would also have been greased with animal fats.

PORTABLE ANTIQUITIES SCHEME

All finders of gold and silver objects, and groups of coins from the same finds, over 300 years old, have a legal obligation to report such items under the Treasure Act 1996. Now prehistoric base-metal assemblages found after 1 January 2003 also qualify as Treasure.

The Portable Antiquities Scheme is a voluntary scheme for the recording of archaeological objects found by members of the public. The scheme was established to promote the recording of chance finds and broaden public awareness of the importance of such objects for understanding our past.

The government recognised that there was an urgent need to improve arrangements for recording all 'portable antiquities' which fell outside the scope of the Treasure Act 1996, and as a result the Portable Antiquities Scheme was established. In 1997 the Department of Culture, Media and Sport provided funding to institute pilot schemes for the voluntary recording of archaeological objects in six regions. Another five pilot schemes were established five years later, funded by the Heritage Lottery Fund. It is hoped to expand the scheme to all parts of England and Wales in due course.

For local offices consult the Portable Antiquities Scheme Website at www.finds.org.uk/index.asp

or write to the head office at:
Portable Antiquities Scheme, c/o dept of Coins & Medals, British Museum, London WC1B 3DG.
Tel: 020 7323 8611

TREASURE TROVE
OF SCOTLAND

Unlike in England, in Scotland all finds, regardless of whether they are metal detector finds or from an archaeological excavation, are subject to assessment. If they are deemed of national importance, they will be claimed by the Crown.

Once the find has been reported there are three possible outcomes:

1) If the find is of limited archaeological or historical interest the object will be returned to the finder.

2) If the find is of some archaeological or historical interest, but is not significant enough to claim as treasure trove, then a certificate of disclaim by the Crown will be issued. The certificate makes clear that the find has been considered but that the Crown is not exercising its right to claim it and the find is being returned.

3) If the find is of significant archaeological or historical interest it will be recommended for claiming by the Crown. The Treasure Trove Advisory Panel will then consider the find at one of its meetings and will advise the Crown Agent to which Scottish museum it should be

allocated. When a find is allocated to a museum it becomes the property of that museum and the finder is normally awarded an *ex gratia* payment equivalent to the find's market value. The finder will be notified which museum the find has been allocated to and the amount of any reward payable.

If finds from an excavation are claimed by the Crown, the excavators will be advised in writing by the Crown Office. Once the decision has been made as to which museum is to be allocated the finds, the excavators will again be advised of this by the Crown Office and the excavators and museum may then make arrangements for the delivery of the finds.

In certain cases, particularly when the fieldwork concerned has been small-scale evaluation, finds may be judged to be of insufficient archaeological interest to be claimed as treasure trove. If this happens the unit or excavator responsible for the fieldwork is issued with a certificate of disclaim by the Crown. The offer of disposal to a local museum may be negotiated where appropriate. This procedure recognises the fact that museums are increasingly wary of a 'blanket' acceptance of all finds, irrespective of their character, from fieldwork.

An important point with regard to all fieldwork finds is that **no reward is payable**, no matter what the nature of the material found. The Crown takes the view that fieldwork is undertaken with the ultimate aim of a better knowledge of Scotland's past and that those who undertake it do so on the understanding that their finds will be housed in museums for the benefit of the nation.

Further details of the processing of fieldwork finds can be found in a booklet produced by the Scottish Executive entitled *Treasure Trove in Scotland: Guidelines for Fieldworkers.* More information can be found on the web at: www.treasuretrove.org.uk/index.html

Alternatively contact the head office at:

Treasure Trove Advisory Panel Secretariat
National Museums of Scotland
Chambers Street
EDINBURGH
EH1JF
Email: info@treasuretrove.org.uk

BIBLIOGRAPHY

Chapter 1

Gold

Aicheson, L. 1960, *A History of Metals, 2 Vols.* Interscience, New York

Callender, R. 1990, *Gold in Britain*. Goldspear, Beaconsfield

Calvert, J. 1853, *The gold rocks of Britain and Ireland*. Chapman and Hall, London. Republished by Goldspear, Beaconsfield.

Morteani, G. & Northover, J.P. (eds.) 1993, *Prehistoric Gold in Europe: Mining, Metallurgy and Manufacture*. Kluwer Academic Publishers, London

Forbes, R.J. 1972, *Studies in Ancient Technology Vol VIII*. E.J. Brill, Leiden

Herrington, R., Stanley, C., Symes, R. 2000, *Gold*. Natural History Museum, London

Hodges, Henry 1964, *Artifacts: An Introduction to Early Materials and Technology*. Duckworth, London

Lewis, P.R. & Jones, G.D.B. 1969, 'The Dolaucothi Gold Mines I: the surface evidence' *The Antiquaries Journal*, XLIX, 244–272.

McClaren, M.J., 1903, *The occurrence of gold in Great Britain and Ireland*. Transactions of the Institute of Mining Engineers, London

Rapson, W.S. 1978, *Gold Usage*. Academic Press, New York

Tylecote, R.F. 1962, *Metallurgy in Archaeology*. Edward Arnold, London

Wayman, M.L. 1989, *All that Glitters: Readings in Historical Metallurgy.* The Metallurgical Society of the Canadian Institute of Mining and Metallurgy, Toronto

Copper

Aicheson, L. 1960, *A History of Metals, 2 Vols.* Interscience, New York

Atkinson, R.L. 1987, *Copper and Copper Mining.* Shire Publications, Aylesbury

Bowen, R. & Gunatilaka A. 1977, *Copper: Its Geology and Economics.* Applied Science Publications, London

Coghlan, H.H. 1975, *Notes on the Prehistoric Metallurgy of Copper and Bronze in the Old World.* Pitt Rivers Museum, Oxford

Copper Development Association, 1960, *Copper Through the Ages.* CDA, London

Day, J. & Tylecote R.F. 1991, *The Industrial Revolution in Metals.* The Institute of Metals, London

Forbes, R.J. 1972, *Studies in Ancient Technology Vol IX.* E.J. Brill, Leiden

Hibben, T. 1944, *The Sons of Vulcan: The Story of Metals.* T. Werner Laurie Ltd, London

Hodges, H. 1964, *Artifacts: An Introduction to Early Materials and Technology.* Duckworth, London

Percy, J. 1861, *Metallurgy Vol. 1 Part 2.* John Murray, London

Tylecote, R.F. 1962, *Metallurgy in Archaeology.* Edward Arnold, London

Wayman, M.L. 1989, *All that Glitters: Readings in Historical Metallurgy.* The Metallurgical Society of the Canadian Institute of Mining and Metallurgy, Toronto

Bronze

Aicheson, L. 1960, *A History of Metals, 2 Vols.* Interscience, New York

Forbes, R.J. 1972, *Studies in Ancient Technology Vol IX.* E.J. Brill, Leiden

Hibben, T. 1944, *The Sons of Vulcan: The Story of Metals.* T. Werner Laurie Ltd, London

Brass

Aicheson, L. 1960, *A History of Metals, 2 Vols.* Interscience, New York

Craddock, P.T. 1990, *2000 Years of Zinc and Brass.* British Museum Occasional Papers 50, London

Day, J & Tylecote, R.F. 1991, *The Industrial Revolution in Metals.* The Institute of Metals, London

Forbes, R.J. 1972, *Studies in Ancient Technology Vol VIII*. E.J. Brill,
    Leiden
Percy, J. 1861, *Metallurgy Vol. 1 Part 2*. John Murray, London
Wayman, M.L. 1989, *All that Glitters: Readings in Historical
    Metallurgy*. The Metallurgical Society of the Canadian
    Institute of Mining and Metallurgy, Toronto

Silver

Aicheson, L. 1960, *A History of Metals, 2 Vols*. Interscience, New
    York
Blair, C. 1987, *History of Silver*. Time Warner Books, London
Forbes, R.J. 1972, *Studies in Ancient Technology Vol VIII*. E.J. Brill,
    Leiden
Hodges, H. 1964, *Artifacts: An Introduction to Early Materials and
    Technology*. Duckworth, London
Percy, J. 1861, *Metallurgy Vol. 3*. John Murry, London
Tylecote, R.F. 1962, *Metallurgy in Archaeology*. Edward Arnold,
    London

Lead

Aicheson, L. 1960, *A History of Metals, 2 Vols*. Interscience, New
    York
Day, J & Tylecote, R.F. 1991, *The Industrial Revolution in Metals*.
    The Institute of Metals, London
Forbes, R.J. 1972, *Studies in Ancient Technology Vol VIII*. E.J. Brill,
    Leiden
Hodges, H. 1964, *Artifacts: An Introduction to Early Materials and
    Technology*. Duckworth, London
Hunt, C.J. 1970, *The lead miners of the Northern Pennines, in the
    eighteenth and nineteenth centuries*. Manchester University
    Press, Manchester
Percy, J. 1861, *Metallurgy Vol. 3*. John Murray, London
Rowe, D.J. 1983, *Lead Manufacturing in Britain: A History Story*
    Routledge Kegan & Paul, London
Tylecote, R.F. 1962, *Metallurgy in Archaeology*. Edward Arnold,
    London
Willies, L. 1989, *Lead and Lead Mining*. Shire Publications,
    Aylesbury

Tin

Aicheson, L. 1960, *A History of Metals, 2 Vols*. Interscience, New
    York
Atkinson, R.L. 1985, *Tin and Tin Mining*. Shire Publications,
    Aylesbury

Day, J & Tylecote, R.F. 1991, *The Industrial Revolution in Metals.* The Institute of Metals, London

Forbes, R.J. 1972, *Studies in Ancient Technology Vol IX.* E.J. Brill, Leiden

Franklin, A.D., Olin, J. & Wertime, T.A. (eds) 1977, *The Search for Ancient Tin.* Smithsonian Institute, Washington DC

Gerrard, S. 2000, *The Early British Tin Industry.* Tempus Publishing, Stroud

Hedges, E.S. (ed) 1960, *Tin and its Alloys.* Edward Arnold, London

Penhallurick, R.D. 1986, *Tin in Antiquity.* The Institute of Metals, London

Tylecote, R.F. 1962, *Metallurgy in Archaeology.* Edward Arnold, London

Pewter

Bett, V. 1981, *Phaidon Guide to Pewter.* Phaidon Press Ltd, Oxford

Charron, S. 1974, *Modern Pewter, Design and Techniques.* David & Co, London

Cotterell, H.H. 1929, *Old Pewter: its Makers and Marks in England, Scotland and Ireland.* B.T. Batsford, London

Cotterell, H.H. 1968, *Old Pewter: Its Makers and Marks in England, Scotland and Ireland.* Charles Scribner's Sons, New York

Cotterell H.H., Riff, A. & Vetter, M. 1972, *National Types of Old Pewter.* The Pine Press, Princeton

Cotterell, H.H. & Heal, A. 1928, *Pewters' Trade Cards*

Hatcher, J. & Barker, T.C. 1974, *A History of British Pewter.* Longman, London

Hornsby, P. 1983, *Pewter of the Western World 1500-1850.* Schiffer Publishing

Hull, C. 1992, *Pewter.* Shire Publications, Aylesbury

International Tin Research Institute 1979, *Working with Pewter.*

Jackson, R. 1970, *English Pewter Touchmarks.* Wallace-Homestead Book Co.

Michaelis, R.F. 1969, *British Pewter.* Bell, London

Michaelis, R.F. 1971, *Antique Pewter of the British Isles.* Bell, London

Moulson, D. & Neish, A. 1997, *An Introduction to British Pewter.* Brewin Books

Peal, C.A. 1971, *British Pewter and Britannia Metal.* Peebles Press, New York

Peal, C.A. 1977, *More Pewter Marks.* Christopher Peal, New York

Peal, C.A. 1983, *Pewter of Great Britain.* Gifford, London

Worshipful Company of Pewterers 1979, *Catalogue of Pewter in its Possession.* Pewterers Hall, London

Iron

Aicheson, L. 1960, *A History of Metals, 2 Vols.* Interscience, New York

Day, J & Tylecote, R.F. 1991, *The Industrial Revolution in Metals.* The Institute of Metals, London

Forbes, R.J. 1972, *Studies in Ancient Technology Vol IX.* E.J. Brill, Leiden

Gale, J. 1877, *The Prehistoric Use of Iron and Steel.* Trübner & Co., London

Hibben, T. 1944, *The Sons of Vulcan: The Story of Metals.* T. Werner Laurie Ltd, London

Hodges, H.1964, *Artifacts: An Introduction to Early Materials and Technology.* Duckworth, London

Tylecote, R.F. 1962, *Metallurgy in Archaeology.* Edward Arnold, London

Steel

Day, J. & Tylecote, R.F. 1991, *The Industrial Revolution in Metals.* The Institute of Metals, London

Hibben, T. 1944, *The Sons of Vulcan: The Story of Metals.* T. Werner Laurie Ltd, London

Hodges, H. 1964, *Artifacts: An Introduction to Early Materials and Technology.* Duckworth, London

Vaizey, J. 1974, *The History of British Steel.* Weidenfeld & Nicolson, London

Glass

Cool, H.E.M. & Price, J. 1995, *Colchester Archaeological Report 8: Roman Vessel Glass from Excavations in Colchester, 1971–85.* Colchester Archaeological Trust Ltd, Colchester

Davidson, S. 2003, *Conservation and Restoration of Glass.* Butterworth Heinman, London

Edwards, Charleen K. 1974, *A Survey of Glassmaking – From Ancient Egypt to the Present.* The University of Chicago Press, Chicago

Forbes, R.J. 1972, *Studies in Ancient Technology Vol V.* E.J. Brill, Leiden

Grose, David 1983, 'The Formation of the Roman Glass Industry'. *Archaeology* 36 (4) July/August

Grose, David 1984, 'Glass Forming Methods in Classical Antiquity: Some Considerations'. *Journal of Glass Studies* Vol. 26 26–34

Hayes, E.B. 1948, *Glass through the Ages.* Pelican, London

Jackson, C.M, Cool, H.E.M. & Wager, Emma C.W. 1998, 'The

Manufacture of Glass in Roman York'. *Journal of Glass Studies* Vol. 40 55–61

Jones, G.O. 1971, *Glass*. Chapman and Hall, Londo

Merrill, N.O. 1989, *A Concise History of Glass*. Village Craftsmen, Princeton

Robertson, R. A. 1969, *Chats on Old Glass*. Dover Publications, New York

Schuler, F. 1959, 'Ancient Glassmaking Techniques: The Molding Process'. *Archaeology* Vol. 12 (1)

Tait, H. 1991, *Glass 5,000 Years*. Harry N. Abrams Inc, New York

. 1980, *A Short History of Glass*. Corning, New York

Bone

Greep, S.J. 1987, 'Use of Bone, Antler and Ivory in the Roman and Medieval Periods' in *Archaeology Bone, Antler and Ivory*. The United Kingdom Institute for Conservation London

Hodges, H. 1964, *Artifacts: An Introduction to Early Materials and Technology*. Duckworth, London

MacGregor, A. 1985, *Bone, Antler, Ivory and Horn: The Technology of Skeletal Materials Since the Roman Period*. Croom Helm Ltd, Beckenham

O'Connor T.P. 1987, 'On the Structure, Chemistry and Decay of Bone, Antler and Ivory' in *Archaeology Bone, Antler and Ivory*. The United Kingdom Institute for Conservation London

Penniman, T.K. 1952, *Pictures of Ivory and Other Animal Teeth, Bone and Antler*. Oxford University Press, Oxford

Antler

Greep, S.J. 1987, 'Use of Bone, Antler and Ivory in the Roman and Medieval Periods' in *Archaeology Bone, Antler and Ivory*. The United Kingdom Institute for Conservation London

Hodges, He. 1964, *Artifacts: An Introduction to Early Materials and Technology*. Duckworth, London

MacGregor, A. 1985, *Bone, Antler, Ivory and Horn: The Technology of Skeletal Materials Since the Roman Period*. Croom Helm Ltd, Beckenham

O'Connor, T.P. 1987, 'On the Structure, Chemistry and Decay of Bone, Antler and Ivory' in *Archaeology Bone, Antler and Ivory*. The United Kingdom Institute for Conservation London

Penniman, T.K. 1952, *Pictures of Ivory and Other Animal Teeth, Bone and Antler*. Oxford University Press, Oxford

Ivory

Beigbeder, C. 1965, *Ivory.* G.P. Putnam, London

Espinoza, E.O. 1991, *Identification Guide for Ivory and Ivory Substitutes 2nd Edition.* The World Wildlife Fund in cooperation with the CITES

Secretariat Washington DC, USA

Greep, S.J. 1987, 'Use of Bone, Antler and Ivory in the Roman and Medieval Periods' in *Archaeology Bone, Antler and Ivory.* The United Kingdom Institute for Conservation London

Hodges, H. 1964, *Artifacts: An Introduction to Early Materials and Technology.* Duckworth, London

MacGregor, A. 1985, *Bone, Antler, Ivory and Horn: The Technology of Skeletal Materials Since the Roman Period.* Croom Helm Ltd, Beckenham

O'Connor T.P. 1987, 'On the Structure, Chemistry and Decay of Bone, Antler and Ivory' in *Archaeology Bone, Antler and Ivory.* The United Kingdom Institute for Conservation London

Penniman, T.K. 1952, *Pictures of Ivory and Other Animal Teeth, Bone and Antler.* Oxford University Press, Oxford

Phillips, P. 1987, *Ivory: A History and Collector's Guide.* Thames and Hudson, London

Ritchie, C.I.A. 1969, *Ivory Carving.* Barker, London

Victoria and Albert Museum 1971, 'The Care of Ivory: Technical Notes on the Care of Art Objects'. *Victoria and Albert Museum 6* London

Wills, G. 1968, *Ivory.* A.S. Barnes and Co, London

Woodhouse, C. P. 1976, *Ivories: A History and Guide.* David & Charles, Newton Abbot

Wood

Earwood, C. 1993, *Domestic Wooden Artefacts in Britain and Ireland from Neolithic to Viking Times.* University of Exeter Press, Exeter

Eaton, R.A. & Hale, M.D.C. 1993, *Wood: Decay, pests and protection.* Chapham & Hall, London

Hodges, H. 1964, *Artifacts: An Introduction to Early Materials and Technology.* Duckworth, London

Rowell, R.M. & Barbour, R.J (eds) 1990, *Archaeological Wood: Properties, Chemisty and Preservation.* American Chemical Society, Los Angeles

Tsoumis, G. 1992, *Science and Technology of Wood: Structure, Properties and Utilization.* Chapman & Hall, London

Taylor, M.1981, *Wood in Archaeology.* Shire Archaeology, Aylesbury

Western, C. 1969, 'Wood and charcoal in archaeology' in
Brothwell, D. and Higgs, E.S. *Science in Archaeology.* (pp. 188–90)

Jet

Allason-Jones, Lindsay 1996, *Roman Jet in the Yorkshire Museum.*
The Yorkshire Museum, York

Bower J.A. 1873, *Whitby Jet and its Manufacture.* Journal of the
Society of Arts, 22, 19 Dec. (pp.80–7)

Kendall, H.P. 1936, *The Story of Whitby Jet.* Unknown, Whitby

Muller, H. 1980, *Jet Jewellery and Ornaments.* Shire Publications,
Aylesbury

Owen, J.S. 1975, 'Jet mining in north-east Yorkshire' *Cleveland
Industrial Archaeologist* 3 (p.18)

Parkin C. 1882, *On Jet Mining.* Transactions of the North
England Institute of Mining Mechanical Engineers XXXI,
(p51-7)

Leather

Cameron, E. (ed) 1998, *Leather and Fur: Aspects of Early Medieval
Trade and Technology.* Archetype, London

Edwards, G. & Mould, Q. 1995, *Guidelines for the care of
waterlogged
Archaeological Leather.* English Heritage (can be downloaded
free from www.english-heritage.org.uk)

Forbes, R.J. 1972, *Studies in Ancient Technology Vol V.* E.J. Brill,
Leiden

Hodges, H. 1964, *Artifacts: An Introduction to Early Materials and
Technology.* Duckworth, London

Leather Conservation Group 1981, *Leather, its Composition and
Changes with Time.* The Leather Conservation Group,
Northampton

Mould, Q., Carlisle, I. & Cameron, E., *Leather and
Leatherworking in Anglo-Scandinavian and Medieval York: The
Archaeology of York. The Small Finds 17/16 Craft, Industry and
Everyday Life.* Council of British Archaeology, York.

Reed, R. 1972, *Ancient Skins, Parchment and Leather.* Seminar
Press, London

Thomas, S., Clarkson, L.A. & Thomson, R. 1983, *Leather
Manufacture Through the Ages.* Proceedings of the 27th East
Midlands Industrial Archaeological Conference, EMIAC 27

Walsall Museum 1993, *Leather Bibliography.* Walsall Leather
Museum, Walsall

Waterer, J.W. 1968, *Leather Craftsmanship.* G. Bell, London
– 1972, *A Guide to the Conservation and Restoration of Objects
Made Wholly or in Part of Leather.* G. Bell, London

Chapter 2

Gunflints

Chandler, R.H. 1918, 'Some Supposed Gunflint Sites'. *PPS East Anglia* 2:360-365

Clarke, R. 1935, 'The Flint-knapping Industry at Brandon'. *Antiquity.* March IX

Clay, R.C.C. 1925, 'A Gun-flint Factory Site in South Wiltshire'. *Antiquaries Journal,* 5:423–426

de Lotbiniere, S. 1971, 'The Story of the English Gunflint, some Theories and Queries' *Journal of the Arms and Armour Society,* 9 (1):18–53

Forrest, A.J. 1983, *Masters of flint.* Brandon Industries, Lavenham

Hamilton, T.M. 1968, Review of 'A History of Gunflints'. *Historical Archaeology;* 3:116–118

Kenmotsu, N. A. 1990, 'Gunflints: A study'. *Historical Archaeology* 24 (2):92–124. Kent, Barry C. 1983, 'More on gunflints'. *Historical Archaeology* 17(2):27–40

Knowles, F. H.S. and Barnes, A. S. 1937, 'Manufacture of Gunflints'. *Antiquity* 12:201–207. 12:201–207

Skertchly, J. 1879, 'On the manufacture of gunflints, the methods of excavation for flint, the age of Palaeolithic man and the connexion between Neolithic art and the gun-flint trade'. *Mem. Geol. Survey England and Wales*

Pebble maceheads

Palmer, S. 1968, 'A Mesolithic Macehead from Portland'. *Dorset Natural History and Archaeological Society,* 89, 119–20

Rankine, W.F. 1949, 'Stone Maceheads with Mesolithic Associations in South-East England'. *Proceedings of the Prehistoric Society,* 70

Rankine, W.F. 1953, 'A Study of quartzite maceheads: Functional interpretation and perforation techniques'. *Archaeological Newsletter,* 4 (12), 86–8

Chapter 3

A guide to pottery forms

Barton, K.J. 1975, *Pottery in England from 3500BC to 1750* AD. David & Charles, London

Brears, P. C.D. 1971, *The English Country Pottery.* Charles E. Tuttle Co., London

Cooper, E. 1972, *A History of Pottery*. St. Martins Press, London
— 1972b, *Ten Thousand Years of Pottery*. British Museum Press, London
Fisher, S. 1965, *English Ceramics*. Hawthorne Books Inc., New York
Honey, W.B. 1949, *European Ceramic Art*. Faber and Faber Inc., New York
Lewis, G. 1969, *A Collectors History of English Pottery*. Viking Press, London
Orton, C; Tyers P. & Vince, A. 1993, *Pottery in Archaeology*. Cambridge University Press, Cambridge
Poole, J.E. 1995, *English Pottery*. Cambridge University Press, Cambridge
Rackham, B. 1924, *English Pottery*. Scribner & Sons Inc., New York
Rye, O.S. 1981, *Pottery Technology: Principles and Reconstruction*. Taraxacum, Washington DC
Shepard, A.O. 1963, *Ceramics for the Archaeologist*. Carnegie Institution of Washington, Washington DC

Care of ceramics

Bradley, S. (eds) 1990, *A Guide to the Storage, Exhibition and Handling of Antiquities*. Ethnographia and Pictorial Art, BMP Occasional Paper No. 66
Buys, S. & Oakley, V. 1993, *The Conservation and Restoration of Ceramics*. Butterworth-Heinemann, Oxford
Cronyn, J. 1990, *The Elements of Archaeological Conservation*. Routledge, London
Oakley, V.L. & Jain, K.K. 2002, *Essential in the Care and Conservation of Historical Ceramic Objects*. Archetype Publications, London
Parsons, C.S.M. & Curl, F.H. 1963, *China Mending and Restoration*. Faber & Faber, London
Payton, R. 1992, *The Retrieval of Objects from Archaeological Sites*. Archetype Publications, London
Sease, C. 1987, *A Conservation Manual for the Field Archaeologist*. UCLA AI Art Volume 4, Los Angeles
Watkinson, D.& Neal, V. 1997, *First Aid for Finds*. Rescue and United Kingdom Institute for Conservation Archaeology Section, 3rd edition

Neolithic pottery

Annable, F.K. & Simpson, D.D.A. 1964, *Guide Catalogue to the Neolithic and Bronze Age Collections in Devizes Museum*. Wiltshire Archaeological and Natural History Society, Devizes

Barton, K.J. 1975. *Pottery in England from 3500BC– 1730 AD.* David & Charles, London

Gibson, A & Woods, 1990, *Prehistoric Pottery for the Archaeologist.* Leicester University Press, Leicester

Gibson, A. 1986, *Neolithic and Early Bronze Age Pottery.* Shire Publications, Aylesbury

Smith, I.F. 1956, *The decorative art of Neolithic ceramics in south-eastern England, and its relations.* PhD thesis, University of London

Bronze Age pottery

Abercromby, J. 1912, *A Study of Bronze Age Pottery of Great Britain and Ireland.* Oxford University Press, Oxford

Barrett, J.C. 1991, 'Bronze Age Pottery and the problem of classification' in Barrett, J., Bradley, R. & Hall, M. (eds) *Papers on Prehistoric Archaeology of Cranborne Chase.* Oxbow Monograph No. 11, Oxford (pp.201–230)

Clarke, D.L. 1970, *Beaker Pottery of Great Britain and Ireland.* Cambridge University Press, Cambridge

Cowie, T.G. 1978, *Bronze Age Food Vessel Urns.* British Archaeological Reports No. 55, Oxford

Gibson, A.M. 1978, *Bronze Age Pottery in the North East of England.* British Archaeological Reports No. 56, Oxford

Gibson, A.M. 1982, *Beaker Domestic Sites: A Study in the Domestic Pottery of the Late Third and Early Second Millennia BC in the British Isles.* British Archaeological Reports No. 107, Oxford

Gibson, A.M. 1986, *Neolithic and Early Bronze Age Pottery.* Shire Publications, Aylesbury

Gibson, A.M., Kinnes, I.A. & Burleigh, R. 1983, 'A dating programme for British Beakers'. *Antiquity,* 57 (pp.218–19)

Longworth, I.H. 1984, *Collard Urns of the Bronze Age in Great Britain and Ireland.* Cambridge University Press, Cambridge

Mercer, R.J. (ed) 1977, *Beakers in Britain and Europe: Four Studies.* British Archaeological Report No. S26, Oxford

Harrison, R.J. 1980, *The Beaker Folk: Copper Age Archaeology in Western Europe.* Thames & Hudson, London

Iron Age pottery

Avery, M. 1973, 'British La Tène decorated pottery: an outline'. *Etudes Celtiques 13-2, Actes du Quatrième Congrès International d'Etudes Celtiques, 2* (pp.522–51)

Barton, K.J. 1975, *Pottery in England from 3500BC–AD 1730.* David & Charles, London

Elsdon, S. 1989, *Later Prehistoric Pottery in England and Wales.* Shire Publications, Aylesbury

Elsdon, S.M. 1975, *Stamp and Roulette Decorated Pottery of the La Tène Period in Eastern England: A Study in Geometric Designs.* British Archaeological Reports No. 10, Oxford

Gibson, A. & Woods, 1990, *Prehistoric Pottery for the Archaeologist.* Leicester University Press, Leicester

Grimes, W.F. 1952, 'The La Tène art style in British early iron age pottery'. *Proceedings of the Prehistoric Society* 18 (pp. 160-75)

Morris E.L. 1995a., 'Study 10: Pottery production and resource locations: an examination of the Danebury collection'. In Cunliffe, B. *Danebury, an Iron Age hillfort in Hampshire Volume 6: A hillfort community in perspective.* Council for British Archaeology Research Report 102 (pp. 239-245)

Roman Samian ware

Bird, J. 1995, 'Third century samian ware in Britain', *Journal of Roman Pottery Studies.* Vol. 6 1-14

Bulmer, M. 1980, *An introduction to Roman samian ware: with special reference to collections in Chester and the North West.* Chester Archaeological Society, Chester

Bushe-fox, J.P. 1913, the use of samian pottery in dating the early roman occupation of the north of Britain' *Archaeologia* 64 (pp. 295-314)

Dore, J. & Greene, K. (eds) 1977, *Roman Pottery Studies in Britain and Beyond.* British Archaeological Reports 30, Oxford

Greene, K.T. 1978, 'Imported fine wares in Britain AD 250: A guide to identification' in *Early fine wares in Roman Britain* ed. Marsh, G.D. & Arthur, P.R. British Archaeological Reports 30, Oxford (pp. 3-60)

Hartley, B.R. 1969, 'Samian ware or terra sigillata' in Collingwood, R.G. and Richmond, I. *The Archaeology of Roman Britain.* Methuen & Co. Ltd, London

Johns, C. 1971, *Aretine and samian pottery.* British Museum Press

Swan, V.G. 1988, *Roman Pottery in Britain.* Shire Archaeology, Aylesbury

Tyers, P. 1996, *Roman pottery in Britain.* B.T. Batsford, London

Walters, H.B. 1908, *Catalogue of the Roman pottery in the Department of Antiquities.* British Museum, London

Webster, G. 1996, *Roman Samian pottery in Britain.* CBA Practical Handbook, London

Anglo-Saxon pottery

Dunning, G.C., Hurst, J.G., Myers, J.N. & Tischler, F. 1959, *Anglo-Saxon Pottery: A Symposium.* Medieval Archaeology, 3, (pp. 1-78)

Evison, V.I. 1979, *Wheel-thrown Pottery in Anglo-Saxon Graves.* Royal Archaeological Institute, London

Kennett, D. 1989, *Anglo-Saxon Pottery.* Shire Publications, Aylesbury

Myres, J.N.L. 1969, *Anglo Saxon Pottery and the Settlement of England.* Oxford University Press, London

Myres, J.N.L. 1977, *A Corpus of Anglo-Saxon Pottery of the Pagan Period: 2 vols.* Cambridge University Press, Cambridge

Mainman, A., *Anglo-Scandinavian pottery from York.* York Archaeological Trust, York

Hurst, J. 1976, 'The Pottery' in Wilson, D. (ed.), *The Archaeology of Anglo-Saxon England.* Cambridge: Cambridge University Press

Medieval pottery

Evison V.I., Hodges, H. & Hurst, J.G. (eds), *Medieval Pottery from Excavations: Studies presented to Gerald Clough Dunning.* John Baker, London

Haslam, J. 1978, *Medieval Pottery.* Shire Archaeology, Aylesbury

Jennings, S. 1992, *Medieval Pottery in the Yorkshire Museum.* The Yorkshire Museum, York

McCarthy, M.R. & Brooks, C.M. 1988, *Medieval Pottery in Britain* AD *900-1600.* Leicester University Press, Leicester

Medieval Pottery Research Group 1998, *A Guide to the Classification of Medieval Ceramic Forms. Medieval Pottery Research Group, Occasional Paper 1.* Medieval Pottery Research Group, London

Mellor, M. 1997, *Pots and People that have shaped the heritage of medieval and later England.* Ashmolean Museum, Oxford

Peacock, D.P.S. 1977, 'Ceramics in Roman and medieval archaeology' in Peacock, D.P.S., *Pottery and Early Commerce.* Academic Press, London (pp.21-33)

Rackham, B., *Medieval English Pottery.* Faber and Faber, London

Stoneware

Gaimster, D. R.M. 1997, *German Stoneware 1200 - 1900: Archaeology and Cultural History.* British Museum Press, London

Gusset, G. 1980, *Stoneware: White Salt-Glazed, Rhenish, and Dry Body.* Minister of Supply and Services Canada, Ottawa

Hamilton, D. 1982, *The Thames and Hudson Manual of Stoneware and Porcelain.* Thames & Hudson, London

Klinge, E. 1996, *German Stoneware.* Rijksmuseum Amsterdam, Amsterdam

Oswald, A. 1974, *Nottingham and Derbyshire Stoneware.* English Ceramic Circle Transaction 9 (2): 140–189

Mansfield, J. 1991, *Salt-Glaze Ceramics: An International Perspective*. A&C Black, London

Mountford, Arnold R. 1971, *The Illustrated Guide of Staffordshire Salt-Glazed Stoneware*. Barrie & Jenkins, Ltd., London

Hildyard, Robin 1985, *Brown Mugs: English Brown Stoneware*. Victoria and Albert Museum, London

Tin glaze earthenware

Carnegy, D. 1993, *Tin-glazed Earthenware*. Radnor

Caiger-Smith, A. 1973, *Tin-Glazed Pottery*. Faber and Faber, London.

Archer, M. 1997, *Delftware: The Tin-Glazed Earthenware of the British Isles: A Catalogue of the Collection in the Victoria and Albert Museum*. The Stationery Office, London

Black, J. 2001, *British Tin-Glazed Earthenware*. Shire Publications, Aylesbury

Britton, F. 1982, *English Delftware in the Bristol Collection*. Sotheby Publications, London

Britton, F. 1987, *London Delftware*. Jonathan Horne, London

Pearlware

Cooper, R.G. 1968, *English Slipware Dishes 1650–1850*. Transatlantic Arts, Inc., New York, New York

Dawson, D. 1979, 'Notes on Bristol Yellow Slipwares', *Post-Medieval Archaeology*, 13:204-205

Erickson, M. and Hunter, R. 2001, 'Dots, Dashes, and Squiggles: Early English Slipware Technology' in Hunter, R., *Ceramics in America*. Chipstone Foundation, Milwaukee (pp.94–114)

Hunter, R. (ed) 2001, 'How Creamware Got the Blues: The Origins of China Glaze and Pearlware', in *Ceramics in America*. Chipstone Foundation, Milwaukee (pp.135–161)

Kybalová, J. 1989, *European Creamware*. The Hamlyn Publishing Group Limited, London

Wondrausch, M. 1986, *Mary Wondrausch on Slipware*. A&C Black, London

Porcelain

Cameron, E. 1986, *Encyclopaedia of Pottery and Porcelain in the nineteenth and twentieth centuries*. Faber & Faber, London

Chaffers, W. 1965, *Marks and Monograms on Pottery and Porcelain 2 Vols*. William Reeves, London

Godden, G.A. 1966, *An Illustrated Encyclopaedia of British Pottery and Porcelain*. Herbert Jenkins, London

— 1968, *The Handbook of British Pottery and Porcelain Marks*. Barrie & Jenkins, London

Haggar R.G. 1960, *The Concise Encyclopaedia of Continental Pottery and Porcelain*. Andre Deutsch, London

Hamilton, D. 1982, *The Thames and Hudson Manual of Stoneware and Porcelain*. Thames & Hudson, London

Hobson, R.I. 1923, *A Guide to English Pottery and Porcelain*. British Museum Press, London

Sandon, Jo. 1989, *The Phillips Guide to English Porcelain of the Eighteenth and Nineteenth Centuries*. Merehurst Ltd, London (reprinted by Premier Editions, London 1993)

Williams, N. 1983, *Porcelain Repair and Restoration: A Handbook*. British Museum Press, London

Dating Pottery Backstamps

Cushion, J.P. & Honey, W.B. 1956, *Handbook of Pottery and Porcelain Marks*. Faber & Faber, London

Chaffers, William 1965, *Marks and Monograms on European and Oriental Pottery and Porcelain*. William Reeves, London

Kybalová, Jana 1981, *Ceramic Marks of the World*. Hamlyn, London

Chapter 4

Roman flue tiles

Betts I.M., 1995, 'Roman tile fabrics', in Phillips, D. & Heywood, B. *Excavations at York Minster, Volume I*. Royal Commission on the Historical Monuments of England, 268-269

Betts I., Black E., & Gower J., 1997. 'A corpus of relief patterned tiles in Roman Britain'. Journal of Roman Pottery Studies. Vol 7

Black, E.W. 1985, 'The Dating of Relief-Patterned Flue-Tiles'. Oxford Journal of Archaeology, 4: 3

Brown, A. 1994, 'A Romano-British shell-gritted pottery and tile manufacturing site at Harrold, Bedfordshire'. *Bedfordshire Archaeology* 21, 19-107

Brodribb, G. 1979, 'A Survey of Tile from the Roman Bath House at Beauport Park, Battle, E. Sussex'. *Britannia* X 139-163

— 1987, *Roman brick and tile*. Alan Sutton, Gloucestershire

Lowther, A.W.G. 'A Study of the Patterns of Roman Flue Tiles and their Distribution'. Surrey Archaeological Society, Research Paper No. 1

McWhirr, A. (ed), 1979, *Roman Brick and Tile: studies in manufacture, distribution and use in the western empire*. British Archaeological Reports International Series 68

Redhead N., 1989, 'Stamped tiles' in Redhead, N. et al, Castleshaw: the archaeology of a Roman fort. The archaeology of Greater Manchester 4

Medieval roof tiles

Atkins C., Tibbles J., & Asquith D., 1987, *The archaeology of a medieval roof tile factory site in Grovehill, Beverley*. Archaeology Unit, Humberside County Architect's Department

Betts I., 1993, 'Ceramic roofing tile', in Schofield, J. *et al* 'Medieval Cheapside'. *London and Middlesex Archaeological Society*, 41 (1990), 221–229

Blair, J. & Ramsay, N. (eds) 1991, *English Medieval Industries*. Hambledon Press, London (pp.211–237)

Drury P., 1981, 'The production of brick and tile in medieval England' in Crossley, D. (ed.) 'Medieval Industry'. *CBA Research Report* 40, 126–39

Egan, G. *et al* 1998, *The Medieval Household Daily Living c1150-1450*. Museum of London, London

Garside-Neville, S., 1995, 'The File-Curved and flanged medieval roof tile'. *Interim: Archaeology in York,* Summer 1995, Vol 20, No. 2, 31-34

Hare J.N., 1991, 'The growth of the roof-tile industry in the later medieval Wessex'. *Medieval Archaeology*, 35, 86-103

Lewis, J.M. 1987, 'Roof tiles: some observations'. *Medieval Ceramics*, 11, 3-14

Schofield, John, Allen Patrick & Taylor, Colin 1990, 'Medieval Buildings and Property Development in the area of Cheapside'. *Transactions of the London and Middlesex Archaeological Society,* Vol 41 221-225

Medieval floor tiles

Degan, S. & Seeley, D. 1988, 'Medieval and Later Floor Tiles in Lambeth Palace Chapel'. *London Archaeology* 6.1 11-18

Eames, E. S. 1980, *Catalogue of medieval lead-glazed earthenware tiles in the department of Medieval and Later Antiquities, British Museum, vol. I & II*. British Museum Publications, London

— 1985, *English medieval tiles*. Harvard University Press

— 1992, *English tilers (Medieval Craftsmen series)*. University Toronto Press, Toronto

Knight S. & Keen K., 1977, 'Medieval floor tiles from Guisborough Priory, Yorkshire'. *Yorkshire Archaeological Journal,* 49, 65-75

Lewis, J. 1976, *Welsh Medieval Paving Tiles.* National Museum of Wales, Cardiff

Mellor M., 1989, 'Medieval tile' in Allen, T.G., 'Excavations at Bury Close, Fawler, Oxfordshire'. *Oxoniensia* LIII 1988 (1989) 309

Nichols, J. G. (ed.). 1998, *Medieval tile designs Examples of decorative tiles, sometimes termed encaustic, engraved in facsimile, chiefly in their original size.* Dover Publications, Mineola, New York

Schofield, J., Allen, P. & Taylor, C. 1990, 'Medieval Buildings and Property Development in the area of Cheapside'. *Transactions of the London and Middlesex Archaeological Society.* Vol 41 225–226

Wight, J. A. 1975, *Mediaeval floor tiles: their design and distribution in Britain.* John Baker, London

Bricks

Brunskill, R.W. 1990, *Brick Building In Britain.* Victor Gollancz Ltd., London

Cox, A. 1979, *Brickmaking: A History and Gazetteer.* Bedfordshire County Council Royal Commission on Historical Monuments (England)

Lloyd, N.A. 1925, *History of English Brickwork.* H. Greville Montgomery, London

Lynch G.C.J. 1990, *Gauged Brickwork: A Technical Handbook.* Gower Technical Press, Aldershot

Woodforde, J. 1976, *Bricks To Build a Brick House.* Routledge & Kegan Paul, London

Glass Wine Bottles

Berry, F. 1935, 'Dated English Wine Bottles', *Country Life,* March 30

Dumbrell, R. 1983, *Understanding Antique Wine Bottles.* Antique Collectors Club, Woodbridge

Dunsmuir R. 1976, 'Old and Rare English Wine Bottles'. *Antique Collector* August

Hedges, A.A.C. 1999, *Bottles and Bottle Collecting.* Shire Publications, Princes Risborough

Lewis, M. 1975, 'Vintage Bottles'. *Art and Antiques,* August 23

Meigh, E. 1972, *Story of the Glass Bottle.* Ramsden & Co., London

Morgan, R., *Sealed bottles, Their history and evolution (1630-1930)*

Price, R. 1908, 'Notes on the Evolution of the Wine Bottle'. *Transactions of the Glasgow Archaeological Society.* Vol 6 225–226

Robertson, W.S., 'A Quantitative Morphological Study of the Evolution of Some Post-Medieval Wine Bottles'. *Science and Archaeology,* 17

Van den Bossche, W. 2001, *Antique Glass Bottles: Their History and Evolution (1500–1850) – A Comprehensive Illustrated Guide With a Worldwide Bibliography of Glass Bottles.* Antique Collectors Club, Woodbridge

Drinking glasses

Bickerton, L.M. 1986, *Eighteenth-Century Drinking Glasses: An Illustrated Guide.* Antique Collectors' Club Ltd, Woodbridge

Charleston, R.J. 1984, *English Glass and the Glass Used in England, circa 400-1940.* George Allen & Unwin, London

Dungworth, D. *The Scientific Study of Glass Working Evidence from 17th and 18th Century Sites in England.*

Tyler, K. *Excavations at John Baker's Vauxhall glasshouse: competing with London's late 17th century market for glass.*

Cutlery and Flatware general

Brown, P. (ed) 2001, *British Cutlery: An Illustrated History of Design, Evolution and Use.* Philip Wilson Publishers Ltd, London

Brown, W.H. 1995, 'Eating Implements'. *Antique Collecting* 29 (9), (pp.21–23)

Cowgrill J., de Neergard, M. & Griffiths, N. 1987, *Knives and Scabbards.* HMSO (Museum of London), London

Hayward, J.F. 1957, *English Cutlery, 16th to 18th Century.* HMSO, London

Himsworth, J.B. 1953, *The Story of Cutlery from Flint to Stainless Steel.* Ernest Benn, London

Hughes, G.B. 1959, 'Evolution of the Silver Table Fork'. *Country Life* 127, (pp.364–5)

Lassen, E. 1960, *Knives and Forks.* Høst & Søn, Copenhagen

Levine, B. 1985, *Levine's Guide to Knives and their Value.* DBI Books Inc. Northbrook, Illinois

Moore, S.J. 1979, 'English Table Cutlery'. *Antique Dealer and Collector's Guide*, May 1979 (pp.64–8) and June 1979 (pp.67–9)

Moore, Simon 2001, *Spoons 1650–1930.* Shire Publications, Aylesbury

Moore, Simon 1995, *Table Knives and Forks.* Shire Publications, Aylesbury

Peterson, Harold L. 1966, *A History of Knives.* Charles Scribner's Sons, New York

Pearce, M. 1979, 'Neglected Cutlery'. *Antique Collecting* 14, (2) (pp.20–22)

Rainwater, D.T. and Felger, D.H. 1976, *A Collector's Guide to Spoons Around the World.* Everybody's Press, Inc. and Thomas Nelson Inc., Publishers, Nashville

Rogers, N.S.H. 1993, 'Knives' in *Anglian and Other Finds from Fishgate: The Archaeology of York, The Small Finds 17/9*. Council for British Archaeology, York (pp.1273–1308)

Rogers, N. & Ottaway, P. 2002, 'Knives' in *Craft, Industry and Everyday Life: Finds from Medieval York*. (pp.2751–2793)

Singleton, H.R. 1973, *A Chronology of Cutlery*. Sheffield City Museums, Sheffield

Smithhurst, P. 1987, *The Cutlery Industry*. Shire Publications, Aylesbury

Spoons

Brown, Peter (ed) 2001, *British Cutlery: An Illustrated History of Design, Evolution and Use*. York Civil Trust, Philip Wilson Publishers, London

Horner, R.F. 1975, *Five Centuries of Base Metal Spoons*

Price, F.G.H. 1908, *Old Base Metal Spoons*. Batsford, London

Hallmarks

Bradbury's Book of Hallmarks. J.W. Northend Ltd, Sheffield

Bunt, C.G. 1897, *Chaffers' Handbook to Hall Marks on Gold and Silver Plate*. William Reeves, London

Culme, John, *The Directory of Gold and Silversmiths, 1838–1914*. London Assay Office Registers

Fallon, John P. 1972, *Marks of London Goldsmiths and Silversmiths, Georgian Period (c1697–1837)*. David & Charles, London

Pickford, Ian (ed), *Jackson's Silver & Gold Marks of England, Scotland and Ireland*. Antique Collector's Club

Hone/whetstone

Ellis, S.E. 1969, 'The Petrology and provenance of Anglo-Saxon and medieval English honestone with notes on some other hones'. *Bulleting of the British Museum (Natural History) Mineralogy* 2, (pp.683–695)

Ellis, S.E. and Moore, D.T. 1990, 'The Hones' in M. Biddle (ed), *Object and Economy in Medieval Winchester*. Winchester Studies 7 ii (p.868–81)

Evison, V.I. 1975, 'Pagan Saxon Whetstones'. *Antiquaries Journal* 55 (pp.70–85)

Moore, D.T. 1978, 'The Petrography and Archaeology of English Honestones'. *Journal of Archaeological Science* 5 (pp.61–73)

Foreman, M. 'The Hones' in Evans, D.H. & Tomlinson, D.G. 1992, *Excavations at 33–35 Eastgate, Beverley, 1983–86 Sheffield*

Excavation Reports 3. Humberside Archaeological Unit, Humberside (p.122)

Mainman, A.J. & Rogers, N.S.H. 2000, ' Hones' in *Craft, Industry and Everyday Life: Find from Anglo-Scandinavian York*. Council for British Archaeology, York

Ottaway, P. & Rogers, N. 2002, *Craft, Industry and Everyday Life: Finds from Medieval York*. The Archaelogogy of York, Small Finds 17/15 Council for British Archaeology, York

Rogers, N.S.H. 1993, 'Hones' in *Anglian and Other Finds from Fishgate: The Archaeology of York, The Small Finds 17/9*. Council for British Archaeology, York (pp.1313–1316)

Bronze Axes

Burgess, C.B. 1964, 'A Palstave from Chepstow with some observations on the earliest palstaves of the British Isles'. *The Monmouthshire Antiquary* 1 (4), 117–24

Burgess, C.B. 1968, *Bronze Age Metalwork in Northern England, c1000 to 700* BC

Burgess, C.B. & Miket, R. (eds) 1979, *Bronze Age Hoards: Some finds old and new*. British Archaeological Reports No. 67, Oxford

Evans, J. 1881, *The Ancient Bronze Implements, Weapons and Ornaments of Great Britain and Ireland*. Longmans, Green and Co., London

Needham, S.P. 1981, *The Bulford-Helsbury Manufacturing Tradition; The production of Stogursey socketed axes during the later Bronze Age in Southern Britain*. British Museum Occasional Paper 13, British Museum, London

Rowlands, M.J. 1976, *The Production and Distribution of Metalwork in the Middle Bronze Age in Southern Britain*. British Archaeological Reports No. 31, Oxford

Roman Leather Shoes

Metcalf, A.C. and Longmere, R.B. 1973, 'Leather Artifacts from Vindolanda'. *Transactions of the Museum Assistants' Group for 1973*. No. 12

Rhodes, M. 1974, 'Leather Footwear' in Jones, D.M., *Excavations at Billingsgate Buildings, Lower Thames Street, London 1974*. LAMAS Special Paper No. 4

Swann, June 1995, 'The Mass Production of Shoes, From BC to 1856'. Lecture given to the Honourable Company of Cordwainers, Oct. 29

Van Driel-Murray, Carol 1987, 'Roman footwear: a mirror of fashion and society' *Recent Research in Archaeological Footwear*. Association of Archaeological Illustrators & Surveyors, Technical Paper No 8

Van Driel-Murray, Carol 2001, 'Footwear in the North-Western Provinces of the Roman Empire', in Goubitz, Olaf, *Stepping through time, Archaeological Footwear from Prehistoric Times until 1800*. Stichting Promotie Archeologie, Zwolle

Saxon and Medieval Leather Shoes

Grew, F. and de Neergaard, M. 1988, *Shoes and Pattens (Medieval Finds from Excavations in London: 2)*. HMSO, London

MacGregor, A. 1986, 'Anglo-Scandinavian finds From Lloyds Bank, Pavement, and Other Sites.' *The Archaeology of York, v. 17 The Small Finds*, fasc. 3. York Archaeological Trust, London

Owen-Crocker, G. R. 1986, *Dress in Anglo-Saxon England*. Manchester University Press, Manchester

Pritchard, F. 1991, 'Small Finds', *Aspects of Saxo-Norman London: 2 Finds and Environmental Evidence*. ed. Alan Vince. (Special Paper 12) London and Middlesex Archaeological Society

Rhodes, J.M. 1980, 'Leather Footwear' in Jones, D.M., *Excavations at Billingsgate Buildings, Lower Thames Street, London*. Lamas Special Paper No. 4 1980 (p.99-128)

Rhodes, J.M. 1975, 'A Glossary of Shoe Terms'. *Transactions Museums Assistants Group 12*

Swann, J. 1995, 'The Mass Production of Shoes, From bc to 1856'. Lecture given to the Honourable Company of Cordwainers, Oct. 29

Swann, J.M. 1975, 'Shoe Fashions to 1600' in Doughty, P.S. (ed) *Museum Assistants' Group Transactions 12*. Department of Urban Archaeology, London

Thomas, S. 1980, *Medieval Footwear from Coventry: A Catalogue of the Collection of Coventry Museums*. Coventry Museums, Coventry

Thornton, J. (ed) 1971, *Textbook of Footwear Manufacture*. Butterworth & Co., London

Thornton, J. 1975, 'The Examination of Early Shoes to 1600' in Doughty, P.S. (ed), *Museum Assistants' Group Transactions 12*. Department of Urban Archaeology, London

Roman brooches

Fowler, E. 1960, 'The Origins and Development of the Penannular Brooch in Europe Proceedings of the Prehistoric Society'. Vol 26 (pp.149–177)

Hattatt, R. 1982, *Ancient and Romano-British Brooches*. Oxbow, Oxford

— 1985, *Iron Age & Roman Brooches*. Oxbow, Oxford

—1988, *Brooches of Antiquity*. Oxbow, Oxford

—1989, *Ancient Brooches and other Artefacts*. Oxbow, Oxford

Hull, M.R. & Hawkes C.F.C. 1987, *Corpus of Ancient Brooches in Britain by the late Mark Reginald Hull. Pre-Roman Bow Brooches,* B.A.R. (British Series) No. 168

Mackreth, D 1973, *Roman Brooches.* Salisbury and South Wiltshire Museum

Bédoyère, Guy de la 1989, *The Finds of Roman Britain.* B.T. Batsford, London (pp.117-123)

Roman zoomorphic buckles

Hawkes S.C. & Dunning, G.C. 1962, 'Soldiers and settlers in Britain, Fourth to Fifth Century: With a Catalogue of Animal-Ornamented Buckles and Related Belt-Fittings'. *Medieval Archaeology* 5 (pp.1–70)

Hawkes S.C. 1974, 'Some recent finds of Late Roman Buckles'. *Britannia* 5, (pp.386–393)

Roman hair pins

Cool, H. 1990, 'Roman metal hair pins from southern Britain', *Archaeological Journal.* 147, 148–82

Crummy, N. 1983, *The Roman Small Finds from excavations in Colchester 1971-9 Colchester Archaeological Report 2.* Colchester Archaeological Trust Ltd, Colchester (pp.19–31)

— 1979, 'A chronology of bone pins'. *Britannia,* 10 157–64

Hair combs

Ambrosiana, K. 1981, 'Viking Age Combs, Comb Makers and Comb Making in the Light of Finds from Birka and Ribe'. *Stockholm Studies in Archaeology* 2

Care-Evans, A. & Galloway, P. 1983, 'The Combs' in A. Care-Evans (ed) *The Sutton Hoo-Ship Burial* Vol. 3 813–832

Dunley, M. 1988, 'A Classification of Early Irish Combs'. *Proceedings Royal Irish Academy,* 88C 341–422

Golloway, P. 1976, 'Note on the description of bone combs'. *Medieval Archaeology* 20, 154--6

MacGregor 1985, *Bone, Antler, Ivory and Horn: The technology of skeletal materials since the roman period.* Barnes and Noble

MacGregor, A. Mainmann, A.J. & Rogers, N.S.H. 2002, 'Combs' in *Bone, Antler, Ivory and Horn from Anglo-Scandinavian and Medieval York: The Archaeology of York: The Small Finds 17/12 Craft, Industry and Everyday. Life* Council for British Archaeology, York (pp.1982–1985)

Riddler, Ian 1990, 'Saxon Handled Combs from London'. *Transactions of the London and Middlesex Archaeological Society,* Vol. 41, 9–20

Rogers, N.S.H. 1993, 'Hair combs' in *Anglian and Other Finds from Fishgate: The Archaeology of York, The Small Finds 17/9*. Council for British Archaeology, York (pp.1388–1405)

Tyler, S. 1986, 'Three Anglo-Saxon Bone Combs from Great Wakering' *Essex Archaeological History*, 17, 170–72

Ampullae

Renaud, J.G. ed 1968, *Rotterdam Papers, A Contribution to Medieval Archaeology*

Spencer 1971, 'A Scallop shell Ampulla from Caiston and Comperable Pilgrim Souvenirs' *LHA* 6 59-66. Lincolnshire History and Archaeology

Mitchiner, M. 1986, 'Medieval Pilgrim and Secular Badges'. Hawkins Publications South Croydon

Clay Pipes

Ayto, E. 1988, 'The versatile clay pipe'. *Society for Clay Pipe Research Newsletter 19*: 11–12.

Cessford, C. 1997, 'Pipe Stems – a neglected resource? Some thoughts from Caerleon. *Society for Clay Pipe Research Newsletter 51*: 50–54

Davey, P. (ed) 1979, *The Archaeology of the Clay Tobacco Pipe I. Britain: the Midlands and Eastern England*. British Archaeological Reports British Series 63, Oxford

— (ed) 1980, *The Archaeology of the Clay Tobacco Pipe III. Britain: The North and West*. British Archaeological Reports British Series 78, Oxford

— 1981 'Guidelines for the processing and publication of clay pipes from excavations'. *Medieval and Later Pottery in Wales 4*: 38–63.

— (ed) 1981, *The Archaeology of the Clay Tobacco Pipe VI. Pipes and Kilns in the London Region*. British Archaeological Reports, British Series 97, Oxford

— (ed) 1982, *The Archaeology of the Clay Tobacco Pipe VII. More Pipes and Kilns from England*. British Archaeological Reports British Series 100, Oxford

— (ed) 1985, *The Archaeology of the Clay Tobacco Pipe IX. More Pipes from the Midlands and Southern England*. British Archaeological Reports British Series 146i and ii, Oxford

— (ed) 1987, *The Archaeology of the Clay Tobacco Pipe X. Scotland* British Archaeological Reports British Series 178, Oxford

Oswald, A. 1975, *Clay Pipes for the Archaeologist*. British Archaeological Reports, British Series 14, Oxford

Dice

MacGregor, A. Mainmann, A.J. & Rogers, N.S.H. 'Dice' in
*Bone, Antler, Ivory and Horn from Anglo-Scandinavian and
Medieval York: The Archaeolgy of York: The Small Finds 17/12
Craft, Industry and Everyday Life.* Council for British
Archaeology, York (pp.1982-1985)

Medieval Keys

Chapman, D.J. 1956, *Medieval Locks and Keys, a Short Account of
Their History and Origin.* Privately printed at Maidstone
College of Art

Egan, G. 1998, *The Medieval Household: Daily Living 1150–1450*
Stationery Office

Eras, V.J.M. 1957, *Locks and Keys Throughout the Ages.* Lips and
Co. (Extensive study of all aspects of the subject. Originally
published in 1941 in the Netherlands as *Sloten en Sleutels
Door de Eeuwen Heen* by Lips, Dordrecht

Hopkins, Albert A. 1928, *The John M. Mossman Collection,* The
General Society of Mechanics and Tradesmen Reprinted
1954 & 1961. (Very comprehensive history of locks and keys)

Monk, Eric 1974 (reprinted 1999), *Keys: Their History and
Collection.* Shire Publications Ltd, Princes Risborough

Pitt-Rivers, Lieut-Gen. 1883, *On the Development and Distribution
of Primitive Locks and Keys.* Chatto & Windus, London

Ward Perkins, J.B., *London Museum Medieval Catalogue 1940.*
Anglia Publishing, 1993

Seal Matrices

HMSO 1978, 1981, 1986, *Catalogue of seals in the Public Records
Office 3 Vols.* Her Majesty's Stationery Office, London

McGuinness, A. & Harvey P.D.A. 1996, *A Guide to British
Medieval Seals.* University of Toronto Press, Canada

Tonnochy, A.B. 1952, *British Museum Department of British and
Medieval Antiquities Catalogue of British seals-dies in the British
Museum.* Trustees of the British Museum, London

Horseshoes

Clark, John 1995, *The Medieval Horse and its Equipment*
Museum of London, London

Cuddeford, M.J. 1975, 'Identifying old horseshoes'.
Buckinghamshire and Berkshire Countryside 16 (August)

Egan, G. & Pritchard, F. 1991, *Dress Accessories, c1150-1450:
Medieval Finds from Excavations in London.* The Stationery
Office, London

Fleming, G. 1869, *Horseshoes and horseshoeing: their origin, history, uses and abuses.* Chapman & Hall, London

Green, C. 1966, 'The Purpose of the Early Horseshoe'. *Antiquity* 40 (December)

London Museum, 1940, *London Museum Medieval Catalogue.* Anglia Publishing, Ipswich

Murray, R.W. 1939, 'Dating Old English Horseshoes'. *Journal of the British Archaeological Association.* Second Series Vol. 3

Murray, R.W. 1927, 'Origin and History of the English Horseshoe' *Proceedings of the Cotteswold Natural Field Club* Vol. 23

Sparkes, I.G. 1976, *Horseshoes.* Shire Publications, Aylesbury

Taylor, H. 1947, 'Ancient Horseshoes'. *Veterinary Journal* April

Ward, G.R. 1939, 'On Dating Old Horseshoes'. *Hull Museum Publications No.* 205, Hull (appeared originally in *The Transactions of the Lancashire and Cheshire Antiquarian Society* 53)

Thimbles

Anne, J. 1979, *Antique and Unusual Thimbles.* Oak Tree Publications, Dublin

Holmes, E.F. 1976, *Thimbles* Gill and Macmillan, Dublin

— 1985, *A History of Thimbles.* Cornwall Books, London

— 1988, *Sewing Thimbles.* Finds Research Group 700–1700, Datasheet 9

Johnson, E. 1982, *Thimbles.* Shire Publications, Aylesbury

— 2003, *Thimbles and Thimble Cases.* Shire Publications, Aylesbury

Lester Thompson, H. 1996, *Sewing Tools & Trinkets: Collector's Identification & Value Guide.* Collector Books

Lundquist, M. 1976, *Thimble Treasury.* Wallace-Homestead Book Co.

— 1987, *Book of a Thousand Thimbles.* Wallace-Homestead Book Co

Mathis, A. 1986, *Antique and Collectible Thimbles and Accessories.* Collector Books

McConnel, B. 1995, *Collector's Guide to Thimbles.* Random House UK Ltd, London

— 1997, *The Story of the Thimble: An Illustrated Guide for Collectors (Schiffer Book for Collectors).* Schiffer Publishing Ltd

Von Hoelle, J.J. 1986, *Thimble Collector's Encyclopedia.* Wallace-Homestead Book Co.

Zalkin, E. 1988, *Zalkins Handbook of Thimbles and Sewing Implements: A Complete Collector's Guide With Current Prices.* Krause Publications

— 1990, *A Collector's Guide to Thimbles.* Wellfleet

— 1986, *Thimble Collector's Encyclopaedia*. Wallace-Homestead Book Co. Illinois

Spindle Whorls

Crummy, N. 1983, *The Roman Small Finds from Excavations in Colchester 1971-9*. Colchester Archaeological Report 2, Colchester Archaeological Trust Ltd

Foreman, M., 'The Spindle Whorls' in Evans, D.H. & Tomlinson, D.G. 1992, *Excavations at 33-35 Eastgate, Beverley, 1983–86. Sheffield Excavation Reports 3*. Humberside Archaeological Unit, Humberside (p. 123)

Oakley, G.E. & Hall, A.D. 1979, 'The Spindle Whorls' in Williams, J.H. *Saint Peter's Street, Northampton, excavations 1973–6*

Rogers, P.W. 1997, 'Spinning'. *Textile Production at 16-22 Coppergate: The Archaeology of York Vol 17: The Small Finds*. Council for British Archaeology, York (pp. 1735-1745)

Bone Skates

Gutman, D. 1995, *Ice Skating, From Axels To Zambonis*. Viking, (Penguin Books) London

Herner, R. 1995, *Antique Ice Skates for the Collector*. Schiffer Book for Collectors, New York

MacGregor, A. 1976, 'Bone Skates: a Review of the Evidence'. *Archaeological Journal* 133: 57–74

Reader, F.W. 1910, 'Notes on a Bone Object found at Braintree, Essex, and on some similar objects found elsewhere'. *Essex Naturalist* Vol. XVI (pp. 82–96)

West, B. 1982, *A Note on Bone Skates from London*. London & Middlesex Archaeology, Vol. 32

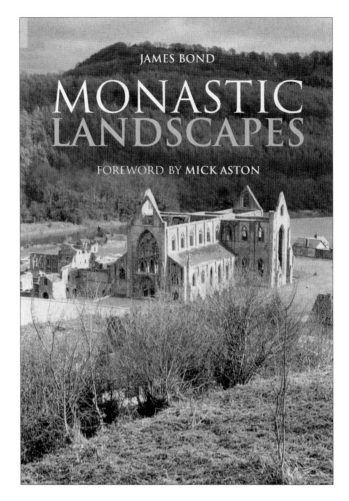

Monastic Landscapes
JAMES BOND

James Bond explores how the church has shaped the landscape we see around us. Many monasteries were endowed with extensive properties, to provide sustenance and income for the community; and as they were often wealthier than secular landlords, they were able to make changes to the surrounding landscape. The author reconstructs, among other features, the towns, villages, agriculture, fisheries and quarries influenced by monastic power.

Archaeological Book of the Year WINNER
'exhaustive coverage and impressive geographical spread, groundbreaking in bringing this topic in a digestible form to a new audience' – British Archaeological Awards' Committee
0 7524 1440 2

If you are interested in purchasing other books published by Tempus, or in case you have difficulty finding any Tempus books in your local bookshop, you can also place orders directly through our website
www.tempus-publishing.com

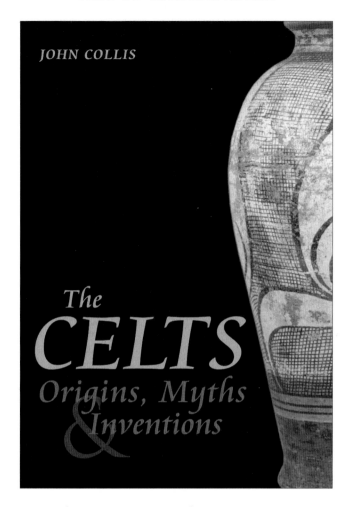

Celts Origins, Myths & Inventions
JOHN COLLIS

We use the word Celtic fast and loose, it evokes something mythical and romantic about our past, but what precisely does it mean? Why do people believe there were Celts in Britain, and what relationship do they have to the ancient Celts? John Collis focuses on how they were reinvented in the sixteenth and later centuries, and argues that this legacy of mistaken interpretations still affects the way we understand the ancient sources and archaeological evidence.

Archaeological Book of the Year RUNNER UP
'exceptional in its European coverage, a major work of synthesis covering the development of this subject area, written in an accessible, personal style, stimulating in its analysis of the archaeological debate and its modern political dimension.' – British Archaeological Awards' Committee

0 7524 2913 2

If you are interested in purchasing other books published by Tempus, or in case you have difficulty finding any Tempus books in your local bookshop, you can also place orders directly through our website

www.tempus-publishing.com

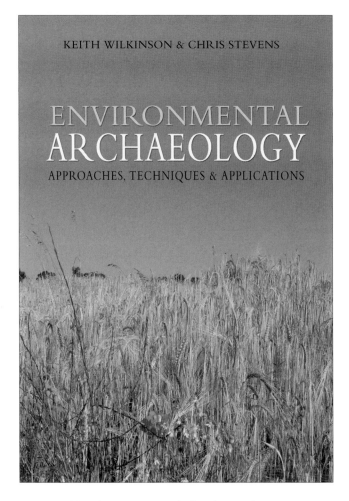

KEITH WILKINSON & CHRIS STEVENS

ENVIRONMENTAL ARCHAEOLOGY

APPROACHES, TECHNIQUES & APPLICATIONS

Environmental Archaeology
KEITH WILKINSON & CHRISTOPHER STEVENS

Two young archaeologists use case studies to introduce environmental archaeology to a non-scientific readership. They provide clear explanations for the many techniques now employed and relate the results of biological/geological studies to modern archaeological theory.

'I am glad to have it on my shelves and reading lists. ... An excellent discussion of aims and objectives. ... The beautiful cover photograph reminds us what environmental archaeology should be about.' – British Archaeology

0 7524 1931 5

If you are interested in purchasing other books published by Tempus, or in case you have difficulty finding any Tempus books in your local bookshop, you can also place orders directly through our website

www.tempus-publishing.com

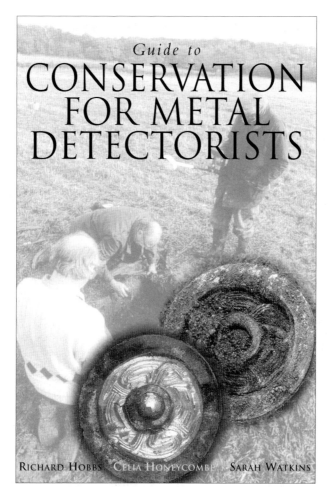

Guide to Conservation for Metal Detectorists

RICHARD HOBBS, CELIA HONEYCOMBE & SARAH WATKINS

Every year thousands of metal artefacts are found by members of the public. However, burial in the ground, often for hundreds of years, means that these metal objects are not as strong as their modern equivalents.

Written by experts for amateurs, this step-by-step guide takes into account the technical considerations that the finder needs to be aware of before interventionist conservation is undertaken.

'A practical guide to handling metal finds in the field and in the home.' – Oxbow Book News

0 7524 2522 6

If you are interested in purchasing other books published by Tempus, or in case you have difficulty finding any Tempus books in your local bookshop, you can also place orders directly through our website

www.tempus-publishing.com

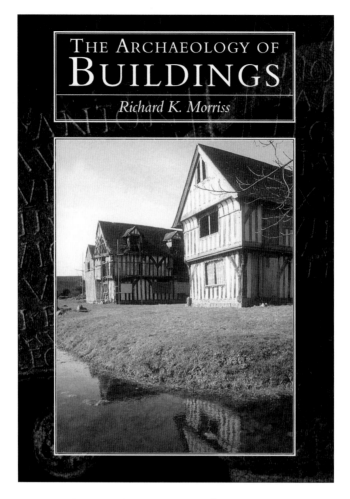

The Archaeology of Buildings
RICHARD MORRISS

This book includes individual sections on specific building materials, to aid understanding of fabrics and construction methods thus enabling the buildings archaeologist to get to grips with the equipment and techniques needed for recording in the field. It goes on to outline how basic documentary sources can add to the historic background and use of the site. With two invaluable appendices – typical examples of buildings archaeology in practice and an illustrated glossary of terms – this is an essential guide book for professionals and amateurs alike.

'*The standard work on surveying standing buildings. … Richard Morriss is our foremost authority. … If there was an award for the best Handbook of the Year, this book would win hands down.*' – Current Archaeology

0 7524 1429 1